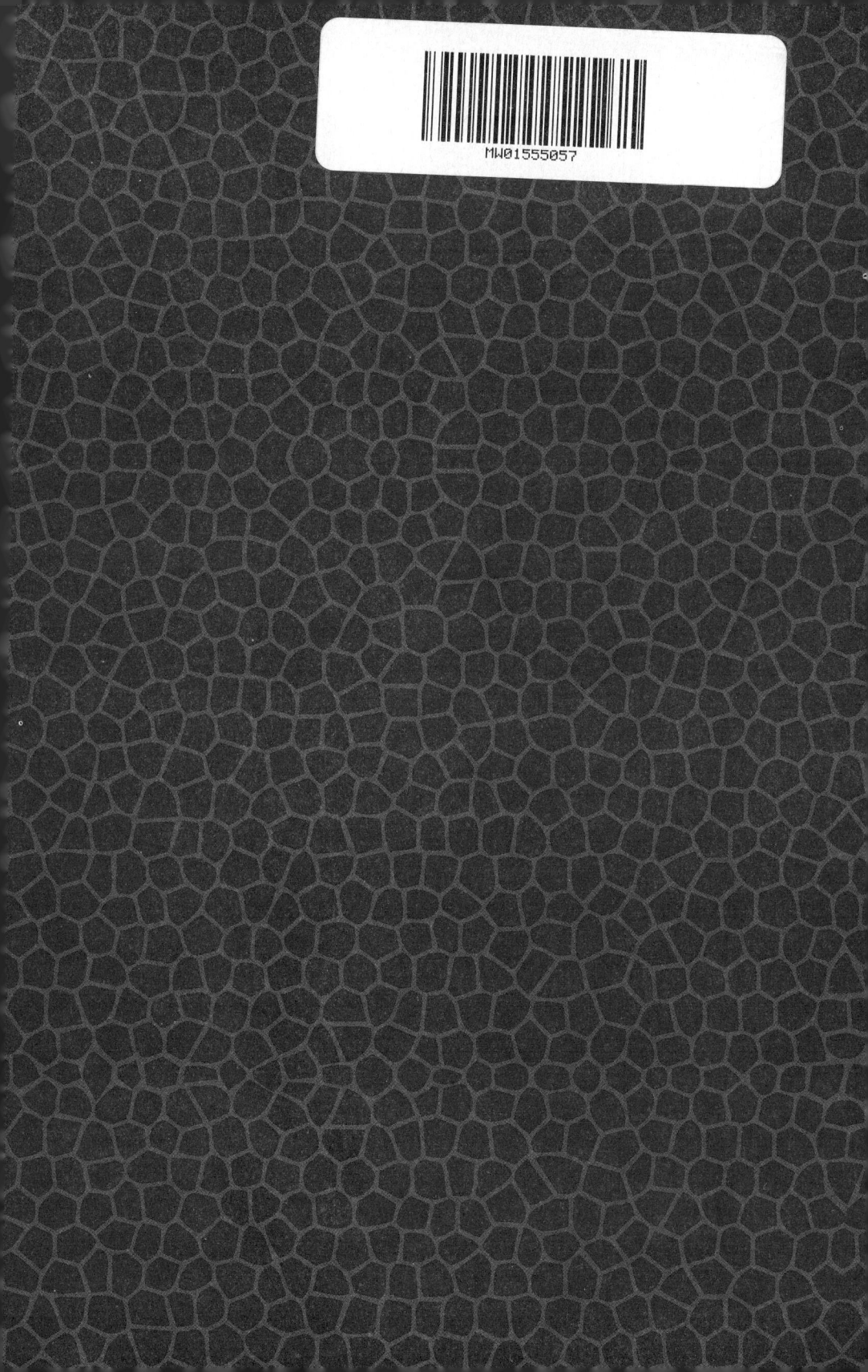

Rav Asher Weiss
on Mo'adim

Bein Ha'metzarim

Rav Asher Weiss
on Mo'adim

Bein Ha'metzarim

Translated by Rabbi Yehoshua Grant
Edited by Rabbi Immanuel Bernstein

Copyright © 2022 by Mosaica Press

ISBN: 978-1-957579-30-6

All rights reserved. No part of this book may be used or reproduced or transmitted in any form or by any means, electronic or mechanical, including photocopying, recording, or by any information storage and retrieval system, without written permission from the publisher.

Published by Mosaica Press, Inc.
www.mosaicapress.com
info@mosaicapress.com

בס"ד

With profound gratitude to

HaRav Asher Weiss שליט"א

for his unparalleled Torah leadership of Klal Yisrael

May his teachings about the Three Weeks
and the fast days instill in us the enormity
of what has been lost, and help to bring about
repentance and redemption, במהרה בימינו.

NICOLE AND RAANAN AGUS AND FAMILY
New York and Jerusalem

Table of Contents

Shiurim

One: The Halachic Foundations of the Fast Days 3

Two: The Principles and Parameters of the Fast of Tishah B'Av. 24

Three: Torah Study on Tishah B'Av. 39

Four: Torah Study When Tishah B'Av or Erev Tishah B'Av
Falls on Shabbos 54

Sichos

Five: As If They Had Destroyed It. 65

Six: I See an Almond Branch 72

Seven: They Did Not Recite a Berachah before Studying Torah. 75

Eight: They Loved Money and Hated One Another 89

Nine: Emunah and Bitachon in Times of Divine Concealment 92

Ten: She Weeps Incessantly at Night 97

Eleven: You Are Children to Hashem Your God 101

Twelve: Fortunate Are You, Rabbi Akiva 105

Thirteen: May It Be Your Will That You Cloak Yourself
in Your Mercy 108

Fourteen: Remove the Evil of Your Ways 111

Fifteen: The Vision of Yeshayahu Ben Amotz I 114

Sixteen: The Vision of Yeshayahu Ben Amotz II 117

Seventeen: In the Great Metropolis of Rome......................120

Eighteen: This Storm Is Because of Me 127

Nineteen: She Has Become Like a Widow 131

Twenty: They Started to Weep, but Rabbi Akiva Laughed 133

Twenty-One: The Keruvim Were Embracing One Another 136

Twenty-Two: Grant Our Portion in Your Torah....................138

Twenty-Three: Do Not Revoke Your Covenant with Us 145

Twenty-Four: And He Is Bound in Chains 149

Twenty-Five: This I Shall Take to Heart 152

Twenty-Six: I Await Him Every Day That He Should Arrive 156

Twenty-Seven: To Open the Paths of Teshuvah.................. 158

Twenty-Eight: With Fire You Are Destined to Rebuild It 160

Twenty-Nine: On Account of Kamtza and Bar Kamtza 164

Thirty: He Proclaimed for Me a Mo'ed.........................185

Thirty-One: Rebbi Sought to Abolish Tishah B'Av 188

Thirty-Two: Comfort, Comfort My People 191

Thirty-Three: Hashem Is the Builder of Yerushalayim..............195

Netzach Yisrael

Thirty-Four: An Address at Auschwitz..........................201

Thirty-Five: Parchment Burning, Letters Ascending 209

Thirty-Six: Remembering the Holocaust 214

Thirty-Seven: Educating Children about the Holocaust............218

Shiurim

ONE

The Halachic Foundations of the Fast Days

I have decided to examine the themes of the various fast days found in the Torah, Chazal, Jewish custom, as well as in the accounts of the conduct of the Sages of the Gemara. I came across approximately thirty-three fast days, concerning which I adduce the opening word of the *pasuk*, "גל עיני ואביטה נפלאות מתורתך—Reveal my eyes and I shall see wonders from Your Torah," which has the numerical value of thirty-three (ג"ל). These fast days may be divided into four categories: repentance, appeasement, mourning, and commemoration.

Repentance

The most common classification is that of repentance, since a fast is an auspicious time for both repentance and atonement. We will provide eighteen sources for this:

1. The most obvious example is Yom Kippur. On this holy and awesome day, we are commanded to afflict ourselves to atone for our sins, as it states:

> And it shall be for you as an eternal statute, in the seventh month, on the tenth of the month, you shall afflict yourselves and all manner of work you shall not do, the citizen and the stranger who dwells among you. For on this day, He shall atone

for you, to purify you from all your sin, before Hashem you shall be purified.¹

2. There is a custom to fast on Erev Rosh Hashanah, as stated in *Shulchan Aruch*,² which is also a fast of repentance.

3. Men of piety and devotion fast throughout the Ten Days of Repentance, as stated by the *Rama*.³

4. There is a custom to fast on Erev Rosh Chodesh, known as Yom Kippur Katan. Yom Kippur Katan is clearly a miniature version of Yom Kippur—a day that is auspicious for repentance. This *minhag* is cited by the *Magen Avraham*.⁴

5. The fasts of BaHaB. The basis for this set of fasts is *Tosafos* to *Kiddushin*,⁵ the *Shulchan Aruch*,⁶ and *Magen Avraham*,⁷ and is based on *Sefer Iyov*, which relates that Iyov was concerned that his children had sinned out of feasting and merriment. The custom therefore arose to fast on Monday, Thursday, and Monday following Sukkos and Pesach, due to the concern of sins having been committed due to excessive rejoicing over the festive period. See also *Orach Chaim* 568.⁸

6. Men of piety and devotion would fast during the days of *Shovavim* (the weeks during which the first six *parshiyos* in *Sefer Shemos* are read), as stated by the *Shelah* and others. This custom is also discussed by the *Biur Halachah*.⁹ These days, too, are auspicious for repentance and atonement, as stated there.

7. The *chevrah kadisha* customarily fast on the seventh of Adar—the yahrzeit of Moshe Rabbeinu—to atone for any lack of respect they may

---

1   *Vayikra* 16:28–29.
2   *Orach Chaim* 581:2; *Yoreh Deah* 214:1.
3   *Orach Chaim* ibid.
4   417:3.
5   81a, s.v. "*Sakva.*"
6   *Orach Chaim* 492.
7   Ibid. 1.
8   2, *Rama*.
9   566:2, s.v. "*V'yesh.*"

have displayed toward the deceased. In fact, the *Shulchan Aruch* states that the seventh of Adar is one of the days on which it is appropriate to fast over certain tragedies that befell our ancestors.[10] However, the *Luach Eretz Yisrael* of Rav Tukachinsky states that *minhag Eretz Yisrael* is that the *chevrah kadisha* fast on this day.

8. The *Shulchan Aruch* states, "It is the practice of the pious to fast on every Erev Shabbos."[11] There are three explanations given for fasting on Erev Shabbos:

1. The *Beis Yosef* states that it is to facilitate eating the Shabbos meal with an appetite. However, this explanation is difficult to understand, for it is only with regard to Erev Pesach that it is stated that a person should refrain from eating a fixed meal, and even there the requirement is only from midday and onward.[12] It would be unusual to act more stringently on Erev Shabbos than the requirement—stated in the Mishnah—to abstain from food on Erev Pesach so as to eat matzah with an appetite.

2. In the *sefer Magen Avos*,[13] the *Meiri* states that on Erev Shabbos it would be customary to review all the Torah one learned during the week, and hence, there would not be time to eat. This is a big *chiddush* and does not sit well with the wording of the *Shulchan Aruch*, which clearly states that this was the practice of pious people. According to the *Meiri*, it was not a practice of pious people but of scholars.

3. The best explanation appears to be that of the *Kaf Hachaim*,[14] citing the *Mekubalim*, that Erev Shabbos, like Erev Rosh Chodesh, is an auspicious time for *teshuvah* and for the atonement of sin. Therefore, the custom arose to fast.

---

10   *Orach Chaim* 560:1.
11   Ibid. 249:3.
12   *Pesachim* 99b.
13   *Inyan* 23.
14   *Orach Chaim* 249:21.

This is also apparent from the *Yerushalmi*,[15] where it states that Rabbi Yochanan would fast every Erev Rosh Hashanah, and Rav Avun would fast every Erev Shabbos. The juxtaposition of these two practices by the Gemara indicates that they share a common theme, namely, *teshuvah* and atonement.

In one place, the *Mishnah Berurah* states that the reason for this fast is to ensure one eats the Shabbos meal with an appetite,[16] whereas elsewhere,[17] he states that Erev Shabbos is a time for *teshuvah*. These two statements can be reconciled, but it is beyond the scope of the present discussion.

Apart from the above, which are fixed public fast days, there are other private fast days, relating to certain events, which carry the theme of *teshuvah* and atonement:

9–10. A *taanis chalom* is a fast undertaken due to a disturbing dream and is codified by the *Shulchan Aruch*.[18] The source of the idea of a *taanis chalom* is the Gemara in *Berachos*,[19] which states that if a person has a bad dream and is distressed about it, he must fast on that day—even if it is Shabbos. In the event that he does fast on Shabbos, he must fast an additional day to atone for his fast on Shabbos. These are thus two further fasts that carry the theme of atonement.

11. A *chassan* and *kallah* fast on their wedding day, as stated by the *Rama*.[20] The source of this *minhag* is a *teshuvah* of the *Maharam Mintz*[21] and a *teshuvah* of the *Mahari Bruna*.[22] The reason for the *minhag* is that a *chassan* is forgiven for all his sins on his wedding day.[23]

---

15 *Taanis* 12b.
16 249:18.
17 250:3.
18 *Orach Chaim* 288.
19 31b.
20 *Orach Chaim* 573:1 and *Even Ha'ezer* 61:1.
21 109.
22 93.
23 As stated in the *Yerushalmi, Bikkurim* 3:3, 11b.

12. A sinner must fast to atone for his sin. This halachah is cited by the *Rama* in several contexts:

1. One who accidentally desecrates Shabbos must undertake four fast days.[24]
2. One who had relations with a *niddah* should fast.[25]
3. One who transgresses the prohibition of *yayin nesech* should fast for five days.[26]

The source for these fasts is *the sefer Rokeach*.

13. Likewise, the *Magen Avraham* rules that if a person finds that the *retzuos* of his tefillin were inverted, he should fast.[27]

14. If a *Sefer Torah* falls to the ground, the entire congregation should fast. The same applies when tefillin fall to the ground, if they are not in their containers. However, in that case, only the person from whose hand the tefillin fell must fast, as stated by the *Magen Avraham*.[28]

I have seen that there is a dispute between two leading Sages as to the basis of this halachah—the *Divrei Chaim* 29 and *Avnei Nezer*.[30] According to the *Divrei Chaim*, the reason for the fast is that when a *Sefer Torah* is disgraced, it is a sign from Heaven that the Attribute of Justice is presiding, and the congregation must repent. The *Divrei Chaim* therefore ruled stringently in a case where a *Sefer Torah* was disgraced by non-Jews who broke into a shul in the middle of the night. However, the *Avnei Nezer* maintains that the idea of the fast is to atone for the sin of having disgraced the *Sefer Torah*. He therefore rules leniently in the case where it was disgraced due to unavoidable circumstances, where no negligence was exhibited.

15. The Gemara states that following a Torah dispute between Rav Huna and Rav Chisda, Rav Huna fasted forty fasts for having upset

---

24   *Shulchan Aruch, Orach Chaim* 334:26.
25   *Yoreh Deah* 185:4.
26   Ibid. 123:26.
27   27:17, based on *Mo'ed Katan* 25a.
28   44:5.
29   *Yoreh Deah* 1:109.
30   Ibid. 2:375.

Rav Chisda, and Rav Chisda fasted forty fasts for having suspected Rav Huna.[31]

16. There is a similar instance recorded in the *Yerushalmi* in which Rav Mana ruled incorrectly with regard to the question of "the *meinekes* of one's fellow."[32] He fasted that entire day as a result.

17. The first person to ever repent was Adam HaRishon, who fasted for 130 years to atone for the sin of the *Eitz HaDaas*, as related by Chazal in *Maseches Eiruvin*.[33]

18. Another fast of repentance recorded by Chazal was undertaken by Rabbi Elazar ben Azaryah, whose cow went out on Shabbos carrying a strap between its horns.[34] The Gemara explains that the cow, in fact, belonged to his neighbor, but the sin was attributed to him because he did not object. The *Yerushalmi* states, "Rabbi Chanania said: [The cow] went out once, yet his [Rabbi Elazar ben Azaryah's] teeth became black from fasting."[35]

A similar account is related regarding Rabbi Yehoshua:

> It was taught in a Beraisa: Rabbi Yehoshua said, "I am embarrassed of your words, Beis Shammai. Is it possible that a woman kneads in her bowl [in the attic of a building that contains a dead body that has an opening to the attic entirely blocked by an earthenware vessel], and the woman and her bowl are impure for seven days, yet the dough is pure? [Is it possible] to have jugs filled with water; and the jugs are impure for seven days, but the water is pure?" One student of Beis Shammai engaged with him and said, "I will tell you the reasoning of Beis Shammai." "Speak," he replied. The student asked, "Does an impure vessel block [the transfer of tumah]?" "It does not," he replied. [The student asked,] "Is the vessel of

---

31   *Bava Metzia* 33a.
32   *Sotah* 19b.
33   18b.
34   *Shabbos* 54b.
35   *Shabbos*, end of chap. 5, 33a.

an am ha'aretz pure or impure?" "Impure," he replied. [The student then said,] "If you tell him that it is impure, will he listen to you? Moreover, if you tell him that it is impure, he will tell you that his is pure and yours is impure—and that is the reasoning of Beis Shammai" [in other words, the Sages did not render it impure since the am ha'aretz would not listen anyway]. Immediately, Rabbi Yehoshua went and prostrated himself upon the grave of Beis Shammai, and declared, "I have been answered for you, bones of Beis Shammai. If such is the case regarding your cryptic statements, all the more so regarding your clear statements!" It was said that throughout his life, Rabbi Yehoshua's teeth were blackened from his fasting.[36]

We see that the greatest Tanna'im fasted many times to atone for sin until their teeth were blackened.

We thus have eighteen examples of fast days with the theme of repentance and atonement.

Appeasement

The second theme of a fast day is that of prayer and appeasement of Hashem. There are nine examples of this type of fast:

1. It is stated that fasts should be proclaimed over every hardship that befalls the Jewish People. This is stated in the first and second chapters of *Maseches Taanis*—if there was no rainfall or if other calamities occurred, they would blow the shofar and fast. This is also discussed at length in the *Shulchan Aruch*.[37]

It would seem that when the Jewish People cry out to Hashem and ask Him for their needs, and appease Him with prayer, supplication, and the sounding of the shofar, they also appease Him by fasting. The Gemara also states that on the days when they would fast over a famine or other crisis, they would investigate the behavior of the townspeople

---

36   *Chagigah* 22b.
37   *Orach Chaim* 575–76.

until midday and then they would pray.³⁸ The Gemara asks why the order was not reversed and answers that it is fitting to pray while fasting, as it states, "With the tribute of the evening I have arisen from my fasting, and I spread out my hands to Hashem." This implies that fasting is a *segulah* for prayers to be answered and to appease the Almighty.

Although the Mishnah states that the elder of the community would say words of rebuke and *mussar* to the people, it nonetheless appears that the fast was one of appeasement, not *teshuvah*.³⁹

2. Another fast of appeasement is that of the *maamad* (shifts of Yisraelim, similar to those of the officiating Kohanim and Leviim), who would fast from Monday to Thursday, and would pray **that the sacrifices of their brethren should be accepted with favor.**⁴⁰

The Gemara states further:

> *The Rabbis taught: The men of the mishmar would pray that the sacrifices of their brothers should be accepted with favor, and the men of the maamad would gather in the beis k'nesses and would observe four fasts: Monday, Tuesday, Wednesday, and Thursday. On Monday—for the sea-travelers; on Tuesday—for those crossing the desert; on Wednesday—that children should not be stricken with diphtheria; and on Thursday—for pregnant and nursing mothers.*⁴¹

We see clearly that they would fast out of prayer and supplication, to arouse Heavenly mercy. Furthermore, the *Yerushalmi* states, "From here they stated that someone who prays and is not answered should fast."⁴² Clearly, fasting is a *segulah* for prayers to be accepted.

3. David HaMelech fasted when his son fell ill, and he prayed to Hashem to cure him.⁴³ The *Shulchan Aruch* therefore rules, "Just as the congrega-

---

38   *Taanis* 13a.
39   Ibid. 15a.
40   Ibid. 26a.
41   27b; see *Biur HaGra* ibid.
42   *Taanis* 2:2, 9a.
43   *Shmuel II*, chap. 12.

tion fast and pray over their difficulties, so should every individual pray and fast over his hardship; for instance, if his son becomes unwell or is imprisoned."[44] It would appear that this is also a fast of appeasement. Although one could argue that it is a fast of *teshuvah*—for it is stated that "repentance, prayer, and charity remove the evil of the decree"—it seems more likely that the fast is one of appeasement. This is implied by the wording of the *Shulchan Aruch*, to "pray and fast." In other words, the fasting serves to accompany the prayer—to appease and supplicate to Hashem, as explained.

4. Many have the custom to fast on the day of their children's wedding. The source of this custom is the *Darkei Moshe*,[45] who states that this was the practice of *Maharash Mi'Ostreich*. It appears that this fast is one of appeasement, during which parents pray that Hashem grant their children a life of happiness and fulfillment and that they should see upright generations. Since we do not find that the sins of the parents are forgiven, it is apparent that the fast of the *chassan* and that of his father have two different themes.

5. The Jewish People would fast when they went out to battle. The *Chayei Adam* states that this is why we fast on Taanis Esther—to emulate the fast conducted by the Jewish People on the thirteenth of Adar when they did battle with their enemies.[46]

The source of this idea is the *Mechilta*:

> "Tomorrow I shall stand…" Tomorrow I shall be with you ready and standing at the top of the hill, as the simple reading implies, says Rabbi Yehoshua. Rabbi Elazar HaModai says: Tomorrow we shall undertake a fast, and shall be supported by the merit of our fathers.[47]

---

44 *Orach Chaim* 578:1.
45 Ibid. 580.
46 155:3, cited by *Mishnah Berurah* 686:2.
47 *Beshalach, Masechta D'Amalek* 1.

The *Mechilta* continues:

> "And his hands were spread out in faithful [prayer] until the sun set." This teaches us that he was fasting—these are the words of Rabbi Yehoshua.

We see that even according to Rabbi Yehoshua, Moshe was fasting. Thus, Moshe fasted when the people went to wage war with Amalek, and the people did likewise on the thirteenth of Adar during the time of Mordechai and Esther. It seems clear that the purpose of this fast is also to appease Hashem, so that He should lead the people to victory, and they should not experience defeat or spoil in their battles.

6. Another example of fasting for appeasement is the set of one hundred fasts conducted by Rabbi Zeira so that he would forget the Torah he learned in Bavel before ascending to Eretz Yisrael. He likewise fasted that Rabbi Elazar should live a long life.[48] It is also recorded that Rav Yosef fasted for many days so that the Torah should not be forgotten from his descendants. We see that fasting is a *segulah* for a person's prayers to be answered. This seems to be a form of appeasement—when a person makes a request of Hashem, it is a *segulah* that he appease Him through fasting.

7. We likewise find that Mordechai and Esther declared a fast at a time of crisis—to annul the decree of Haman and Achashveirosh. Their fasting and supplications were intended to appease Hashem so that their prayers be answered, and to annul the cruel decrees of their enemies.

8. It would seem that this was also the basis for Rabbi Tzadok's forty year fast that the Beis Hamikdash not be destroyed.[49]

9. See also the *Yerushalmi* in *Maseches Kilayim*,[50] which relates that Rabbi Yose fasted for forty days and Reish Lakish for three hundred days that Rabbi Chiya should appear to them in a dream.

---

48 *Bava Metzia* 85a.
49 See *Gittin* 56a.
50 42b.

Mourning

There are four different fasts for which the principal theme is that of *aveilus* (mourning):

1. The four fasts that the Neviim instituted over the *churban Beis Hamikdash*, as it states:

> *The fast of the fourth [month] and the fast of the fifth [month], the fast of the seventh [month] and the fast of the tenth [month], will become for the Jewish People [times of] gladness and joy and days of festivity.*[51]

They proclaimed a fast on these days out of mourning for the *churban*. The *Tashbetz* asserts that only Tishah B'Av relates to *aveilus*, but not the other three fasts.[52] However, it seems clear that the four fasts share a common theme, for the Navi grouped them together in the *pasuk* above. It is just that Tishah B'Av is more stringent as it recalls the culmination of the *churban*, and the destruction of the First and Second *Batei Mikdash*. The intent of the *Tashbetz* is that the **laws** of mourning only apply to Tishah B'Av, but he agrees that the **theme** of all of the four fast days is *aveilus*. This is evident from the fact that the Navi groups them together, as stated, and the fact that it is prophesized that these days will all become times of gladness and joy, implying that today they are times of grief and mourning.

It is also apparent from the Rishonim that the four fast days share a common theme. The *Ramban* states that in the original institution of the Neviim, the five manners of affliction that we observe on Tishah B'Av applied to each of the four fast days.[53] However, later, during the time of the Second Beis Hamikdash, they were lenient regarding the other fasts. The *Tosafos Yeshanim* in *Megillah* takes the opposite approach, namely, that the Neviim only instituted that fasting be conducted on the four fast days, as the *pasuk* states, "The *fast* of the fourth…," but

---

51 Zechariah 8:19.
52 2:271.
53 *Toras Ha'adam*.

after the second *churban*, they instituted an additional stringency for Tishah B'Av as the calamities were compounded; thus, they forbade all five afflictions. At any rate, we see that both the *Ramban* and *Tosafos Yeshanim* agree that no distinction was made in the enactment of the different fasts; they have the same parameters.

It thus seems clear that each of the four fasts are rooted in *aveilus*. This is also stated by the *Tosafos Yom Tov* in his commentary to the beginning of the fourth chapter of *Taanis*.

2. Another fast relating to *aveilus* is the fast conducted on one's parent's yahrzeit, as stated by the *Shulchan Aruch*.[54] The obvious purpose for this fast is to **mourn** one's deceased father.

However, this is not necessarily the case. The *Leket Yosher* cites his *rebbi*, the *Terumas Hadeshen*, who explains that the idea of fasting on the day of a father's yahrzeit is because the son's *mazal* is weakened, and because he is judged each year on the day of his father's passing.[55] If so, the theme of the fast is one of *teshuvah* or *ritzuy*, and should therefore be grouped together with the other fasts of that sort. However, the *Sefer Chassidim* states that since a father and son are considered to be one, a father's yahrzeit is a day of pain for his son.[56] This implies that the theme of this fast is pain and mourning. This is also the simplest approach.

3. The *Shulchan Aruch* states that we fast on days when tragedies and hardships befell the Jewish People, such as the death of *tzaddikim* or the burning of *Sifrei Torah*.[57] These days are also fasts of mourning. Although a mourner is not required to fast, it is nonetheless apparent that these fasts were instituted due to mourning.

It would not be reasonable to say that the *mazal* of the Jewish People is weakened on all the days on which tragedies befell them, for this is only stated regarding Tishah B'Av and the day on which a person's

---

54   *Orach Chaim* 568:7–9.
55   2, p. 98, *inyan* 1.
56   231.
57   *Orach Chaim* 580.

father died. It would be far-fetched to say that this idea also applies to other days on which difficult events took place.

4. In *Sefer Shoftim*, regarding the battle between the tribe of Binyamin and the other tribes, the *pasuk* states:

> And Binyamin went out toward them from the valley on the second day, and they struck another eighteen thousand men from the Jewish People to the ground, all of them wielders of the sword. And all the Jewish People and the entire nation went up and came to Beis El, and they cried and repented there before Hashem, **and they fasted on that day until the evening**, and they offered burnt-offerings and peace-offerings before Hashem.[58]

We see that after the Jewish People suffered defeat in battle and forty thousand men were killed (the *pesukim* state that another twenty-two thousand were killed), they sat, cried, and fasted.

This fast also seems to have been an expression of pain and mourning over those who were slain by the sword.

The *Chasam Sofer* asserts that there are no fast days that relate to mourning.[59] Rather, the theme of every fast is *teshuvah*, as stated by the *Rambam* with regard to the four fast days:

> There are days on which all of Yisrael fast because of the tragedies that occurred on them, to arouse the hearts and to open up the paths of teshuvah, and serve to remind us of our evil actions, and of the deeds of our fathers, which were akin to our actions today, causing these tragedies to befall both them and ourselves. For by remembering these matters we will return to proper conduct, as the pasuk states (Vayikra 26:40), "And they shall confess their sin and the sin of their fathers."[60]

---

58 20:25–26.
59 *Orach Chaim* 208.
60 *Hilchos Taanis* 5:1.

The position of the *Chasam Sofer* is clear—a mourner is not required to fast over his father or mother or any other relative. There is thus no connection between mourning and fasting.

However, ultimately, the *Chasam Sofer* rejects this position. He argues that although no fast was instituted for a mourner in general, we see nonetheless that a person sometimes fasts due to *aveilus*. Therefore, there is, in fact, a notion of a fast of *aveilus*, and it is indeed the theme of these fasts. He also suggests that a fast was not instituted for a mourner in general because the mourning period is seven days, and a person cannot fast for that long.

Certainly, if we are struck by tragedy and we mourn, we must repent, as the *Rambam* states.[61] Nonetheless, the **reason** for these fasts is *aveilus*, though their **purpose** is *teshuvah*.

There appears to be proof for this concept from the *Yerushalmi*, which records a doubt as to whether Tishah B'Av is considered a *taanis tzibbur*.[62] The question discussed by the Gemara is whether we should recite the twenty-four berachos that are recited on a *taanis tzibbur* declared over famine on Tishah B'Av. The *Korban Ha'eidah* and *P'nei Moshe* both explain that the doubt is whether we consider Tishah B'Av a fast of mourning, or if it is like the other public fasts, which are primarily about prayer and supplication, and thus we recite the twenty-four berachos.

We see that the basic assumption of the *sugya* is that there are certainly fasts that carry the theme of *aveilus*.

Commemoration

The fourth classification of fasts is commemoration.

1. This theme is mentioned with regard to Taanis Esther, as the *Rambam* states, "It is the custom of all Yisrael at this time to fast on the thirteenth of Adar, to commemorate the fast that they fasted at the time of Haman, as it states, "The matters of the fasts and their supplication."[63]

---

61   Ibid. 5:1.
62   *Rosh Hashanah* 3:4, 16b.
63   *Hilchos Taanis* 5:5.

We see that Taanis Esther is a commemoration of the fast that took place during the time of Haman.

However, I note that although all agree that Taanis Esther is commemorative, there is still a dispute among the Rishonim as to whether it commemorates the fasting or the miracle. The *Rambam* holds that it commemorates the fast that took place during the time of Haman, as stated. However, the *Ran* cites the *Raavad* who holds that Taanis Esther commemorates the **miracle** of Purim.[64] In this light, the *Ran* explains how we may fast on this day given that it is mentioned as a day of joy in *Megillas Taanis* ("the Day of Nikanor"). The answer is that this fast commemorates a miracle, thus it is permitted to fast though it is forbidden to say a *hesped*. The *Ran* appears to hold that a fast day is never something that is commemorated—we only fast in order to commemorate the miracle, so as to offer thanks to Hashem.

With that said, it seems obvious that a fast day is not simply instituted to commemorate a miracle, for what connection is there between a fast and a miracle? Moreover, we only find commemorative measures that are similar in nature to the miracle itself, such as the Chanukah candles, which commemorate the miracle of the jug of oil in the *Menorah*, or the feasting and rejoicing of Purim. Why then, should we conduct a fast to commemorate a miracle?

We must say that even the *Raavad* agrees that the fast of the thirteenth of Adar is due to the fact that a fast was observed in the time of Mordechai and Esther, which we commemorate. In other words, it seems more logical that the *Rambam* and *Raavad* agree that the *direct* reason for the fast is to commemorate the fact that our ancestors fasted at that time. However, the *initial* reason—meaning the reason that this fast was enacted as a commemorative measure—was to commemorate the miracle.

We may draw a proof to this approach from the comments of the *Rosh* in *Maseches Taanis*: "The practice to fast on the thirteenth of Adar…when they gathered and stood for their lives in battle, and

---

64 *Taanis* 18b.

prayed for mercy, and that too was one of the main elements of the miracle."[65] The *Rosh* states similarly in the first *perek*,[66] citing Rabbeinu Tam who explains that Taanis Esther is based on the notion invoked at the beginning of *Maseches Megillah* that the thirteenth of Adar "is a time of gathering for everyone." We see that the day commemorates the fact that the Jewish People gathered and stood up for their lives in prayer, which was among the main aspects of the miracle.

A similar concept is stated by the *Levush*:

> *They accepted it as an obligation and a public fast in all respects, for on that day, during the time of Mordechai and Esther, they gathered to do battle and stand up for their lives, and they needed to pray for mercy with supplication and entreaty, and they presumably also fasted on that day...and because we celebrate Purim to commemorate that miracle, we must also conduct ourselves as they did regarding the fasting, prayers, and supplication, for would we accept the good and not the bad?!*[67]

We see that we observe the fast to commemorate the fast that took place because we want to commemorate the miracle that occurred; the fast and the miracle go hand in hand.

This raises the following question. The *Rambam* rules that on a fast day, a person should not be joyous and happy, but in a state of sadness and worry.[68] If the fast commemorates a miracle it should surely be a time of joy!

Perhaps the answer is that this only applies to a fast that is connected to distress, as the *Rambam* implies. On Taanis Esther, which commemorates the miracle and is not connected to mourning or calamity, we are not instructed to be sad and mournful. Although we recite the prayer of *Aneinu*, this does not mean that the day is a sad one; rather, since we are

---

65 2:24.
66 *Siman* 1.
67 686:2.
68 *Hilchos Taanis* 1:14.

fasting it is appropriate to arouse Heavenly mercy and ask Hashem to save us from all our troubles. However, since it is not a day of pain and mourning, perhaps there is no mitzvah to be sad and troubled.

The *Ritva* in *Maseches Megillah* contends that the rule "we do not advance times of tragedy" does not apply to Taanis Esther, for the fast does not relate to tragedy but to *teshuvah*.[69] However, this does not appear to contradict our main premise, for I have already argued that all the fast days contain an element of *teshuvah*. The *Ritva*'s main point is that there is no aspect of mourning and pain, not that it is a day of *teshuvah*. See also the *Meiri* in *Maseches Taanis*,[70] who states that Taanis Esther contains an element of joy. Additionally, see the *Magen Avos* on the *Meiri*, which states that Taanis Esther is "a fast of joy," and "it contains an element of prayer and publicizing of the miracle—to give thanks and praise to Hashem over the miracles and mighty acts."[71]

2. Another fast that is commemorative is that of the firstborn on Erev Pesach. *Tosafos* state that the firstborn assumed the custom to fast on this day.[72]

There are also two approaches to understanding this fast. The *Rosh* writes that it commemorates the miracle.[73] However, the *Kol Bo* states that the firstborn Jews in Egypt would offer sacrifices to idols, and when they were redeemed, they fasted to atone for their sin.[74] To commemorate that fast, it became the custom for the firstborn to fast, even today. There are thus two approaches as to whether this fast is to commemorate a miracle or to commemorate a fast, as was the case with Taanis Esther, as explained above. It also seems logical to say that the same approach we took to explaining Taanis Esther similarly applies to Taanis Bechorim, in other words, that both the *Rosh* and *Kol Bo*'s approach stem from the same point.

---

69   5b.
70   18a.
71   *Inyan* 23.
72   *Pesachim* 108a, s.v. "*Rav Sheshes*," based on *Maseches Sofrim* 21:3.
73   *Pesachim* 10:19.
74   58.

However, after analyzing the wording of the *Kol Bo*, I saw that his intent is unclear:

> There is a custom to redeem the firstborn on Erev Pesach, as Rabbeinu David ben Rabbeinu Levi states. Perhaps this custom is due to the fact Hashem redeemed them during the plague of the firstborn. The Yerushalmi relates that their custom is that the firstborn would fast on Erev Pesach. The Rav [with whom the Kol Bo was corresponding] already noted that the reason for the plague of the firstborn was that the priests of idolatry were the firstborns, as per the original practice that [religious] service was performed by the firstborn, and this possibly also applied to the other nations. It is possible that many of the Jews at that time were among the sinners, as the Navi prophesized…nonetheless, Hashem had mercy on them and saved them, and therefore commanded us to redeem them.

It is unclear if the *Kol Bo*'s intent is to explain why we redeem the firstborn or to explain the basis of the *minhag* mentioned in the *Yerushalmi* that the firstborns fast on Erev Pesach. (Presumably, he is referring to *Maseches Sofrim*, rather than the *Talmud Yerushalmi*.)

Clearly, all of the classifications of fasts mentioned thus far are interconnected. When we fast over a lack of rain, we must bring ourselves to repentance by our fasting. Likewise, the purpose of the four fasts of mourning is to open our hearts to *teshuvah*, as the *Rambam* states in *Hilchos Taanis*. Even on Taanis Esther—which is entirely commemorative—we must still arouse ourselves to repent, as the *Ritva* states. Thus, there is always a connection between fasting and *teshuvah*. However, it appears that in terms of their essential definitions, these fasts are predicated on four different principles, as we have explained.

We noted that Taanis Esther and Taanis Bechorim have the same parameters. However, in a practical sense they are observed differently. Whereas everyone fasts on Taanis Esther, it is common practice for *bechorim* to attend a *siyum masechos* and then eat and drink freely after that. This seems puzzling.

In fact, the *Teshuvah Me'ahavah* opposed this practice, ruling that even someone who actually completed a *maseches* on Erev Pesach from his regular study should postpone his *siyum* to another day so as to fast on Erev Pesach.[75] He bases this ruling on a *teshuvah* of the *Maharam Mintz*, which states that a person completing a *maseches* may delay his *siyum* until an appropriate time.[76] In this case, argued the *Teshuvah Me'ahavah*, it would be appropriate to postpone the *siyum* and to fast on Erev Pesach. He relates that in his youth, he raised this issue with the *Noda B'Yehudah* and the *Gra"ch Fishels*.

However, it has already become the widespread practice for *bechorim* to attend a *siyum* and then eat and drink. This is recorded by Rabbi Akiva Eiger,[77] the *Shoel U'Meishiv*,[78] and *Mishnah Berurah*.[79]

It appears to me that in our generation, the practice is not to observe any private fast, even those that are mentioned by the *Shulchan Aruch*. We see that people do not observe a *taanis chalom*, and many do not fast on a yahrzeit. Rabbi Akiva Eiger, in his *tzavaah*, asked of his children not to fast on his yahrzeit, but to spend the day studying Torah. We do not find that our elder rabbis would fast when someone in their household was sick. It is possible that in this vein, the practice is to also be lenient regarding Taanis Bechorim, which is not a fast for everybody—only the firstborn.

However, since Taanis Bechorim is unlike the others fasts, in that all the firstborns are required to fast on a specific day, which is not the case regarding the other private fasts, it became accepted to attend a *siyum* before eating.

3. The *beis din* would not eat on a day that they sentenced someone to death.[80] They derived this from the *pasuk* "Do not eat over the blood."[81]

---

75   2:261; 3:376.
76   119.
77   Manuscript ed., 34.
78   *Yoreh Deah* 399.
79   470:10.
80   *Sanhedrin* 63a.
81   *Vayikra* 19:26.

See the *Rambam* and *Maggid Mishnah*, who state that this is a Torah obligation.[82]

Determining the essence of this fast day needs consideration. It may relate to *teshuvah*, in that *beis din* must entertain thoughts of *teshuvah* out of concern that they erred in judgment, and God forbid caused innocent blood to be spilled. It is also possible that they are meant to pray that the death of this person should atone for him, in which case their fast is one of appeasement. It is also possible that they are meant to feel pain over the death of a Jew for his sin, and they therefore fast out of a sense of mourning. We do not know the secrets of Hashem — whatever the reason, they were obliged to fast.

With that said, I was in doubt as to whether the *beis din* are permitted to drink on this day. The wording of the *Rambam* is that "they may not **eat** that entire day," which seems to imply that they were permitted to drink. The wording of the Gemara is "they may not **taste**." In *Berachos*, the Gemara derives from this *pasuk* that a person may not taste anything before praying, but we are lenient with regard to drinking.[83] Though we do not have to say that these two halachos have the same parameters, it is possible that the fast of the *beis din* does not have the status of a fast at all; the prohibition is only to eat, not drink.

In fact, there is another reason to say that this does not have the parameters of a fast day, for it is only stated that they could not eat **after** they decreed his death sentence; they were permitted to eat before they passed the verdict. This is stated explicitly by the Gemara in *Megillah*,[84] which rules that if a person is to be judged on Chol Hamoed (on which it is forbidden to fast since there is a mitzvah to rejoicing on the festival), the judges eat and drink the entire day, and pass the verdict close to sunset. This is also stated by the *Rambam*.[85] We see that the prohibition to eat only applies after the *beis din* passes the verdict, thus it clearly does not constitute a *taanis*.

---

82 *Hilchos Sanhedrin* 13:4.
83 10b.
84 14b.
85 Loc. cit. 5.

Having explained, based on many sources, that there are four classifications of fasts, it appears that they all have one unifying concept—*tzaar* (distress). Though a person is usually meant to be in a state of joy—"A goodhearted person is as at a feast always"[86]—nonetheless, there are times when it is appropriate to feel *tzaar*, and there are events that call for a person to cause himself to feel *tzaar*. This is the common denominator of all of the fasts.

A person who repents for his sin should feel distress. The same applies to one mourning for a relative. Likewise, a person who comes to supplicate and appease Hashem should feel *tzaar* in the knowledge that he may not be worthy.

Nonetheless, it does appear that there are four different classifications of fast, as explained above.

---

86   *Mishlei* 15:15.

TWO

The Principles and Parameters of the Fast of Tishah B'Av

The Rabbis taught: All mitzvos that apply to a mourner apply on Tishah B'Av. It is forbidden to eat, drink, anoint oneself, wear [leather] shoes, or engage in marital relations, and it is forbidden to read Neviim and Kesuvim, and to study Mishnah, Gemara, Midrash, halachos, and Aggados.

Taanis 30a

Two Aspects of Stringency

There are two areas in which Tishah B'Av is the most stringent of the four fast days relating to the *churban*: (1) in its laws of mourning, and (2) in the severity of the fast. On Tishah B'Av, we are required to observe the five manners of affliction that do not apply to the other fasts. The *Tashbetz* states:

> *Tishah B'Av has an additional dimension that does not exist with regard to the other fasts—which applies even during a time of shemad (religious persecution). This is due to the obligation of mourning; thus, it is forbidden to eat meat or drink wine, as well as other laws that apply to a mourner. The implication is that these laws are specific to Tishah B'Av alone, due to mourning for the churban. It is only because these laws were taught with regard to Tishah B'Av that the [other] laws are taught in relation to Tishah B'Av as well.[1]*

The *Tashbetz* alludes to an explanation for why the aforementioned Gemara in *Taanis* states that the prohibition of eating and drinking on Tishah B'Av is related to mourning—surely a mourner is not required to fast? The answer is that the aspect of mourning is manifested specifically in the prohibition of eating **meat** and drinking **wine** while the prohibition of partaking of any other food is shared by all fast days and is not based on mourning. (The *Radvaz's* comments are discussed in *Minchas Asher, Mo'adim*.[2] We explain that although the theme of each of the four fasts is *aveilus*, the *laws* of *aveilus* only apply to Tishah B'Av).

On the other hand, it is apparent from the *Shulchan Aruch* that the halachos of Tishah B'Av were designed to be like those of Yom Kippur: "The night of Tishah B'Av has the same status as the day regarding all matters, and the prohibition to eat begins while it is still day, and [all its prohibitions] are forbidden during twilight, like Yom Kippur."[3] It states further that pregnant women and nursing mothers must fast—or later compensate for the fast—of Tishah B'Av as they are required to do on Yom Kippur.[4] The source of this halachah is the Gemara in *Pesachim* 54b.

We see that Tishah B'Av is more stringent than the other fasts in two areas: (1) the laws of mourning apply to it, and (2) its halachos are like those of Yom Kippur.

---

1   2, 271.
2   2:36.
3   *Orach Chaim* 553:2.
4   554:5.

I noticed that a significant detail emerges from the Rishonim, namely, that when the Neviim originally instituted the fasts, there was no distinction between the laws of Tishah B'Av and those of the other fasts. The *Tosafos Yeshanim* state:

> There is a difficulty—how could this Tanna have supposed that Rebbi wished to abolish Tishah B'Av entirely? Surely, it is stated (Taanis 30b) that whoever eats and drinks on Tishah B'Av will not see the consolation of Yerushalayim! Further, a beis din cannot contravene the words of a previous beis din unless they are greater in both wisdom and number! The [answer] can be suggested—that he only wished to abolish the added severity that it carries over the other fasts, **for the earlier generations only decreed that it should be a fast day and no more.**"[5]

However, the *Ramban* disagrees.[6] He contends that the Neviim originally instituted **all five manners of affliction on each of the four fasts**. However, during the period of the Second Beis Hamikdash, when the Shechinah returned to its abode and the Jewish People returned to their land, a leniency was made with regard to the other three fasts and only eating and drinking was forbidden.

Both *Tosafos* and the *Ramban* agree that according to the original institution of the Neviim, there was no distinction between any of the fasts. There is a dispute, however, as to whether the original decree was more stringent and the Sages in subsequent generations were lenient, or the reverse.

It would seem that the dispute between *Tosafos* and the *Ramban* has a halachic ramification. If a person feels weak while fasting on Tishah B'Av and assesses that if he were to wash himself with cold water, he would feel better and not need to break his fast, would we allow him to do so? According to the *Tosafos Yeshanim*, the Neviim only forbade eating and drinking. Therefore, although Chazal subsequently forbade

---

5   Megillah 5b, s.v. "*U'bikesh.*"
6   Toras Ha'adam, p. 243 (Mossad HaRav Kook ed.), cited by *Beis Yosef* 550.

all five afflictions, they do not have the same severity as that which the Neviim forbade. It would thus be preferable that he wash himself and not break his fast.

However, according to the *Ramban*, all the five manners of affliction were instituted by the Neviim. It is thus logical to assume that there would be no preference between the two options, and he may do as he wishes.[7]

However, upon reflection, it appears that even the *Ramban* would agree that the prohibition of eating and drinking is more stringent. This is evident from the very fact that a leniency was only granted for other manners of affliction on the other fasts. Moreover, the prohibition of eating and drinking is more stringent even on Yom Kippur, as some maintain that the other afflictions are only Rabbinically prohibited; and all agree that they do not carry the punishment of *kareis*. At any rate, the distinction between the afflictions is only in their level of stringency; there is no halachic difference between them on Tishah B'Av. Therefore, being that all five afflictions were collectively instituted by the Neviim on Tishah B'Av with no distinction drawn between them, it seems that we would not apply the rule that *we waive the most lenient prohibition first* (meaning that we would urge a person to violate one of the other afflictions before that of eating or drinking—"*ha'kal kal techilah*"), and a person may do as he wishes. This matter requires further study.

Another pertinent question is whether, in this case, the act of washing would constitute *taanug*, "pleasure," which is forbidden, or whether it is more comparable to a case of a person who has a wound on his head, where there is no prohibition of washing at all? A further consideration is whether the rule *ha'kal kal techilah* applies to Rabbinic laws. Additionally, should we be concerned that even if he were to wash himself, he would still need to drink, and as such, he would risk violating two prohibitions? There is much more to discuss regarding this topic;

---

7   Elsewhere, I have elaborated on the question of whether drinking a *chatzi-shiur* is more stringent than washing with a full *shiur*.

I only raise it here to sharpen the distinction between the respective opinions of *Tosafos* and the *Ramban*.

The Fast of Tishah B'Av Night

There is a remarkable *chiddush* in the *sefer Nezirus Shimshon*.[8] The author asserts that if a person's state of health is such that he would be unable to fast for a full twenty-four hours, he should eat on the night of Tishah B'Av so as to be able to fast during the day, for the daytime fast is more stringent than the night.

I do not know his basis for contending that the main part of the fast is the day and fasting at night is secondary. Perhaps it is due to the fact that the other fasts only begin at dawn, which indicates that the daytime is the principle time for fasting. However, this seems unconvincing as one cannot compare Tishah B'Av to the other fasts. With regard to the other fasts, the Chachamim never included the nighttime in their enactment. Tishah B'Av, however, was established as a fast of both night and day—like Yom Kippur.[9] Why then, would we distinguish between the night and the day? (The inference the author makes from the *Rambam* in *Hilchos Taanis* 3 is weak, as is apparent to one who examines the matter closely.)

However, the *Nezirus Shimshon's* position may be supported by the *Tosafos Yeshanim*,[10] who maintain the Neviim originally instituted Tishah B'Av to be like the other fasts; in other words, only as a fast, as the *pasuk* states, "The **fast** of the fourth [month], the **fast** of the fifth [month]..."[11] Only after the second *churban* were the Neviim more stringent and instituted the five afflictions on Tishah B'Av. If so, it would appear that the night of Tishah B'Av was not originally equated with the day, for all of the fasts, including Tishah B'Av, were instituted with equal severity—as a daytime fast alone. Subsequently, however, the fast of Tishah B'Av was extended to include the nighttime, in the same way as the five afflictions were added. In this light, the day of

---

8 *Orach Chaim* 554.
9 As stated by the *Shulchan Aruch*, based on *Pesachim* loc. cit.
10 *Megillah* 5b.
11 *Zechariah* 8:19.

Tishah B'Av would indeed be more stringent than the night, for the day of Tishah B'Av has the status of *"divrei kabbalah,"* whereas the night is only *"divrei sofrim."*

However, according to the *Ramban*, each of the four fasts were instituted with a prohibition of the five manners of affliction, and included a nighttime fast, but their severity was relaxed during the period of the Second Beis Hamikdash. His opinion is cited by the *Ran* and the *Beis Yosef*.[12] He states explicitly that this development was also true with regard to fasting at night—in other words, the nights were originally included in all four fasts, but were subsequently subtracted from the obligation. According to his view, there is no distinction between the night and the day of Tishah B'Av, as I have explained.

There is an additional *chiddush* in the ruling of the *Nezirus Shimshon*. Even if we were to accept that the night was more lenient than the day, one could still argue that a person must fast for as long he is able to and that he should not be permitted to commit a transgression now out of concern for the future. On the following day, when the need arises, he may eat legitimately. Why then would we allow him to eat on the night of Tishah B'Av, which is a time when it should essentially be forbidden for him to do so given that he is not yet in *sakanah* (danger)?

There is a similar dispute among the Acharonim regarding a person who would be unable to fast on both Tzom Gedaliah and Yom Kippur. The *Eishel Avraham* rules that he must fast on Tzom Gedaliah.[13] If he is subsequently in a state of *sakanah* on Yom Kippur, he could then eat justifiably—but we can deal with that question if and when it becomes relevant. The *Ohel Moshe* disagrees, ruling that we would allow him to eat on Tzom Gedaliah so that he would be able to fast on Yom Kippur.[14] See also *S'dei Chemed, Maareches Yom Kippur*, in this regard.[15]

However, there is room to suggest that even the *Eishel Avraham* would rule differently in our case in which a person is choosing between eating

---

12 *Orach Chaim* 550, see there.
13 Ibid. 602.
14 16.
15 1:10.

on either the night or day of Yom Kippur. Since both options relate to the same fast of Tishah B'Av, it would make more sense to be lenient during the night to facilitate fasting during the day.[16] A similar concept is stated in *Menachos* 48a—namely, that we allow a person to violate Shabbos to gain something for Shabbos observance, but we would not allow him to violate Shabbos to gain something for the week.

Elsewhere, I have discussed the case of a *chassan* and *kallah* in whose week of *sheva berachos* falls a *taanis tzibbur*, and who would find it difficult to fast twice within such a short time (having fasted on the day of their wedding). Should they forgo fasting on their wedding day, which is only an Ashkenazic custom,[17] so that they will be able to fast on the *taanis tzibbur*, or would we say, "Let the trouble occur in its time"?

There is a further dispute among the Acharonim regarding a prisoner who is allowed out of jail for one day. The question is, should he leave on the first available Shabbos so as to daven with a minyan and hear *k'rias haTorah*, or should he wait until *Shabbos Zachor*, or until Rosh Hashanah so as to hear the shofar, etc.? The *Radvaz* and *Chacham Tzvi* disagree over this question; their views are cited by the *Be'er Heitev*.[18]

Nonetheless, a distinction can be made between this and our case, as is apparent to anyone who analyzes the matter. Further elaboration on this point is beyond the scope of the present discussion.

The Five Afflictions on Tishah B'Av

A fundamental question may be raised with regard to the five afflictions of Tishah B'Av. The two contexts in which these prohibitions generally appear in the Torah are in the laws of mourning and the laws of Yom Kippur. As such, we may ask whether the reason these halachos apply on Tishah B'Av is due to the laws of mourning or due to the comparison between Tishah B'Av and Yom Kippur.

Some Acharonim maintain that there are in fact two dimensions to the prohibition of washing on Tishah B'Av: one pertaining to mourning,

---

16 See *Menachos* 48a for a similar idea.
17 Cited by the *Rama, Orach Chaim* 573, and *Even Ha'ezer* 61.
18 90:11.

and the other to the comparison between Tishah B'Av and Yom Kippur.[19] They prove this from the fact that a mourner may dip his finger in water, whereas on Tishah B'Av this is forbidden,[20] even though the mourning of an individual is usually more stringent than communal mourning. This indicates that the prohibition of washing on Tishah B'Av has two components. It is forbidden to wash due to mourning, but there is an added stringency of not even dipping one's finger in water, which stems from the comparison of Tishah B'Av to Yom Kippur.

This approach has an important halachic ramification in a case discussed by the *Poskim*.[21] If Tishah B'Av coincides with Shabbos and the fast is postponed to Sunday, should the laws of mourning be observed privately on Shabbos? The view of the *Shulchan Aruch* is that Tishah B'Av is entirely postponed, as if it were originally instituted on the tenth of Av, and as such there is no obligation to observe mourning privately on Shabbos. However, the *Rama* maintains that it is only the laws of fasting and mourning that are postponed until after Shabbos — the essence of the day itself is not postponed, and therefore the obligation of mourning in private still applies. According to the *Rama* (whose view we follow) that we observe mourning in private, would it be permissible to wash one's body on that Shabbos (obviously, in a manner that is permitted on Shabbos)? If the institution of the five afflictions was as an added dimension of stringency to the fast itself due to its equivalence with Yom Kippur, when the fast is postponed, the other laws would seemingly be postponed as well. However, if the prohibition of washing stems from the aspect of mourning, it is possible that this would still apply in private, even though the fast is postponed. Therefore, if we would accept that the prohibition of dipping one's finger in water — even a small part of one's body — stems from the comparison to Yom Kippur, we would allow a person to wash his face, hands, and feet in private.

---

19 *Minchas Chinuch*, mitzvah 313; *Chiddushei HaGriz*, beginning of *Hilchos Taanis*.
20 *Orach Chaim* 554:7.
21 554:19.

This being said, it appears that even according to the *Rama*, the obligation of private mourning only applies to marital relations—which are inherently private, but not to washing.

In fact, our question is already discussed by the Rishonim. The *Ritva* asks why Chazal forbade washing one's finger on Tishah B'Av, seeing as this does not apply to a mourner.[22] He answers that they were lenient with regard to a mourner because the mourning period is seven days, and not even washing one's finger for that length of time would prove to be a source of great discomfort—a decree that the community would be unable to abide by. Tishah B'Av, however, only lasts for one day, and as such, it is appropriate to be stringent in this regard, due to the state of mourning. In addition, perhaps the mourning of the entire Jewish nation is treated more stringently. At any rate, we see that even when faced with this question, the *Ritva* did not suggest that there are two aspects to the prohibition against washing, as the Acharonim contend.

However, there seems to be a basis for the *Acharonim*'s position from the *Rambam*:

> That which you must know **is that all the mitzvos that apply to a mourner apply on Tishah B'Av**, *and these laws of mourning will be explained in their place,* **and the laws of its fast are the same as the laws of the fast of Yom Kippur,** *meaning that there is a prohibition of washing, anointing, wearing leather shoes, and marital relations; and we begin the fast on the previous day, and the performance of work on this day is very disgraceful.*[23]

The *Rambam* seems to imply that the prohibition of the five afflictions is due to the comparison with Yom Kippur. See also the Gemara in *Taanis*,[24] which states that whoever eats and drinks on Tishah B'Av is like one who eats and drinks on Yom Kippur.

---

22   *Taanis* 13b.
23   *Peirush HaMishnah*, end of *Maseches Taanis*.
24   30b.

However, I find it difficult to accept that there are indeed two separate aspects here; and in reality, there is no unequivocal proof to this approach from the *Rambam*, for several reasons:

- It appears to me that there is an error in the citation and translation of the *Rambam*, and the correct reading should be: "For all the mitzvos...and it will further be explained in its place, meaning the prohibition of washing...and the laws of its fast are the same as the laws of the fast of Yom Kippur...and we begin the fast on the previous day." This way the words of the *Rambam* would make sense—with each statement in its proper place.
- Even according to the existing version of the *Rambam*, it is clear that he means to lay down two principles, namely, that whatever applies to a mourner applies on Tishah B'Av, and that Tishah B'Av has the same laws as Yom Kippur. He then explains the halachos that result from these principles, respectively: the five afflictions—which are an expression of mourning—and beginning the fast on the previous day—which is an aspect of Yom Kippur.
- However, it would seem that there is already a source for these two dimensions of Tishah B'Av in Chazal. The Gemara at the end of *Taanis* clearly implies that the five afflictions observed on Tishah B'Av are expressions of mourning, yet in *Pesachim*, the Gemara states that a person may not dip his finger in water as on Yom Kippur. This halachah is also stated by the *Rambam*,[25] from which the *Griz* proves that there are indeed two aspects to the prohibition, as explained above.

Nevertheless, it appears more logical to say that the root of the halachos of Tishah B'Av is an expression of *aveilus*, but at the same time, **the laws of Tishah B'Av are like those of Yom Kippur** in severity. And just as on Yom Kippur it is forbidden to eat and drink and to dip one's finger in water, the same is true on Tishah B'Av. If so, it should not surprise us that the *Rambam* puts these two principles together and states in one sentence, first, that all the laws that apply to a mourner etc., and

---

25 *Taanis* 5:10.

second, that the fast is equivalent to Yom Kippur, which is the reason that it is forbidden to wash.

Both of these approaches must contend with the fact that when Chazal would declare a fast day due to a lack of rainfall or a public crisis, during which the five afflictions are forbidden, as stated by the *Rambam*,[26] they nevertheless did not forbid washing one's face, hands, and feet.[27] According to the *Minchas Chinuch* and *Griz*—that dipping one's finger in water is not forbidden due to the aspect of *aveilus* but was prohibited on the each of the fast days that carry a prohibition of washing—why does that not apply to these fasts? Even according to the *Ritva*, it is difficult to explain why Chazal were lenient in this regard, given that it was a fast of a single day and would have been an enactment that the people could uphold.

We must say that since these fasts were instituted according to the order of *BaHaB* (Monday-Thursday-Monday), Chazal did not wish to be stringent regarding washing a small area of the body with cold water. Furthermore, it is possible—even according to the *Ritva*—that they were only stringent in a case when the entire Jewish People mourn for one day. This matter requires further study.

Another point to consider is that according to some Rishonim, only the first day of mourning is *mi'd'Oraisa*. Following the logic of the *Ritva*, the stringencies of mourning should have then been instituted at least on the Torah-ordained first day! In response to this, we must say that Chazal did not want to differentiate between the days of mourning. At any rate, the aforementioned position of the Acharonim is a *chiddush*, which requires further analysis.

The Laws of a Choleh on Tishah B'Av

A question arises with regard to the equating of Tishah B'Av with Yom Kippur: does the comparison extend to the actual parameters of the fast itself? Regarding Yom Kippur, it is stated that a *choleh* (sick person) whose life is in danger—who is permitted to eat—may only eat less

---

26   Ibid. 3:4.
27   See *Shulchan Aruch, Orach Chaim* 575:3.

than a *shiur* (the measure of food that incurs a punishment if eaten) when possible. Moreover, the *Rashba* contends that after the *choleh* has eaten what he needs and is no longer in danger, it is forbidden for him to continue eating, and if he does so, he would be liable to *kareis*.[28] The question is, do these halachos apply to Tishah B'Av?

The *Shulchan Aruch* rules: "A woman within thirty days of childbirth, and similarly, a *choleh* who must eat, does not require evaluation—rather, we give them to eat immediately, for Chazal never decreed [the fast] in a case of illness."[29] The *Mishnah Berurah* explains that the words "does not require evaluation" mean that a person in this state does not require evaluation as to whether the fast would place him in danger,[30] and Chazal never made their decree even with regard to a sick person who is not dangerously ill. The implication of the words, "a *choleh* **who must eat**" is that sick people whose illness does not compel them to eat—like many sick people today who take medication on a regular basis but are not otherwise inhibited by their illness—are obligated to fast once they have taken their medication that allows them to function normally. The fast was only waived for those sick people who must eat as a result of their illness.

Some infer from the *Shulchan Aruch* that in a case of sickness, Chazal did not institute the fast at all; in other words, the fast is completely waived with respect to a *choleh*.[31] Therefore, he would not be required to eat less than a *shiur* or abide by similar restrictions. However, the *Biur Halachah* cites the *Pischei Olam*, who ruled that in areas where the cholera outbreak of his time had not taken hold, people should eat and drink less than a *shiur*.[32]

However, it appears that the halachah does not concur with this view; there is no requirement for a *choleh* to eat less than the *shiur* on Tishah B'Av. This is implied first from the fact that the *Shulchan Aruch* and *Rama* both make no mention of this halachah, whereas they do

---

28   *Kiddushin* 21b, s.v. "*Rav*."
29   *Orach Chaim* 554:6.
30   Ibid. 12.
31   See *Chiddushei HaGrach* 45 and *Aruch Hashulchan, Orach Chaim* 554.
32   *Orach Chaim* 554:6.

mention it with regard to a *choleh* on Yom Kippur.³³ (The *Chazon Ish* states, "This was characteristic of the way of the Rishonim…it was their foremost duty to explain [their teachings] and provide basis for them. [Therefore] their omission is like an admission that the matter is [to be understood] in its simple form, without further detail. And in my opinion, this is the strongest proof."³⁴ The *Beis Meir* expresses a similar sentiment in a *teshuvah* recorded in *Binas Adam*.³⁵)

Furthermore, it seems clear that the ruling of the *Pischei Olam* was not addressed to cholera patients themselves, who were in a state of *sakanah*. Rather, it referred to healthy people who lived in the area who were required eat to protect themselves from contracting the disease. Since they were healthy at the time, the principle that Chazal waived the *taanis* in **a case of sickness** would not apply. They were thus required to eat less than a *shiur*.

After citing the *Pischei Olam*, the *Mishnah Berurah* concludes, "This should be the response to a person who asks—namely, that in this regard, the fast was not entirely uprooted, and Hashem desires the heart." This implies that a *choleh* should attempt to eat less than a *shiur*. However, it would seem that this is not strict halachah, but appropriate conduct by which to fulfill the mitzvah of Chazal, so as not to uproot the fast completely. Although such a person is, in principle, not required to fast at all, nonetheless, "Hashem desires the heart"—thus, a God-fearing person ought to be stringent and eat less than a *shiur*. To my mind, this is apparent from the *Mishnah Berurah*'s expression, "This ought to be the response," meaning that this is not strictly required but should be the conduct of a person who wishes to fulfill his duty in the optimum way. For this reason, he concludes that "Hashem desires the heart." Moreover, if one examines his wording closely, he only cites this ruling as an aside, as an appended note.

The *sefer Shemiras Shabbos K'Hilchasah* cites Rav Shlomo Zalman Auerbach, who suggests that the requirement to eat less than a *shiur*

---

33   *Orach Chaim* 618:7–8.
34   *Sheviis* 7.
35   *Shaar Hakavua* 7.

on Yom Kippur stems from the obligation of *inuy* (affliction).³⁶ Though eating a *chatzi-shiur* is still a Torah prohibition, the *inuy* is not nullified until a full measure has been eaten. If this is correct, this would only apply to Yom Kippur, not to Tishah B'Av, which does not carry the obligation of *inuy*. In the *Miluim* of the *sefer*, the author cites Rav Shlomo Zalman, who quoted the comments of the *Netziv* in *Meromei Sadeh*,³⁷ that according to the view that eating a *chatzi-shiur* is a Torah prohibition, a person would violate the mitzvah of *inuy* in doing so.

One remaining question is whether a *choleh* who ate and revived himself should then continue fasting or whether he has no further requirement to fast given that the fast has already been uprooted.

The *Chasam Sofer*³⁸ discusses whether a *choleh* who needed to eat on Tishah B'Av can receive an *aliyah* at *Minchah* (as the *Shulchan Aruch* states, "There is an opinion that a person who is not fasting may not be called up to the Torah on a *taanis tzibbur*"³⁹). He cites several reasons to be lenient, permitting him to receive an *aliyah*. First, the source of this halachah is the *Teshuvos Maharik* in reference to the fasts of *BaHaB*, which are not distinctive days in and of themselves.⁴⁰ Rather, one who fasts, fulfills the mitzvah of the Sages, but for someone who does not, it remains a regular day. On Tishah B'Av, by contrast, even if a person cannot fast due to illness, it still remains the day of *churban Beis Hamikdash*, which was established as a *taanis*. Therefore, even if a person is required to eat for medical reasons, he does not lose the chance to participate and remains obligated in the Torah reading of the day.

The *Chasam Sofer* provides a further basis for leniency from the fact that a person who needs to eat on Tishah B'Av still remains obligated in the other four afflictions. Since he is still involved in the halachos of the day, he has not lost out and may receive an *aliyah*.

Third, the *Chasam Sofer* suggests that the aforementioned ruling of the *Shulchan Aruch* was only issued for the other fasts, as a person

---

36 39:15.
37 *Yoma* 73a.
38 *Orach Chaim* 157.
39 Ibid. 566:6.
40 *Shoresh* 9.

who does not fast on those days has lost the entire *taanis*. On Tishah B'Av, however, a *choleh* is required to minimize what he eats as much as possible; in other words, he is still commanded to fast and is not considered to be excluded from the group of those who are fasting. The *Maharam Shick* endorses the view of his *rebbi*, and rules that a *choleh* who is required to eat on Tishah B'Av may only eat as much as he requires, no more.[41]

We can conclude from their rulings that even a person who eats on Tishah B'Av to protect his life, and who, strictly speaking, need not have eaten less than a *shiur*, must nonetheless continue fasting once he has eaten what he requires. Therefore, with regard to our question as to whether Tishah B'Av has the same parameters as Yom Kippur, it is apparent that they are only partially comparable. On Tishah B'Av, a *choleh* does not have an obligation to eat less than a *shiur* (it is only a stringency), unlike Yom Kippur. However, the obligation of a *choleh* who has already eaten to resume fasting on Tishah B'Av is subject to dispute among the Acharonim, as outlined above. At least according to the *Chasam Sofer*, Tishah B'Av has the same status as Yom Kippur in this regard, and the *choleh* must resume fasting.

---

41   *Orach Chaim* 289.

THREE

Torah Study on Tishah B'Av

Reasons for the Prohibition

The *Shulchan Aruch* rules: "It is forbidden to read Torah, *Neviim*, and *Kesuvim*, or to study Mishnah, Gemara, halachos, and Aggados, because it is stated, 'The teachings of Hashem are just; they gladden the heart.'"[1]

The *Shulchan Aruch* clearly states that the reason Torah study is forbidden on Tishah B'Av is because Torah gladdens the heart and thus negates the feelings of mourning on Tishah B'Av. However, the *Maharsha*[2] contends that the main reason Torah study was forbidden on Tishah B'Av was to avoid a person being distracted from mourning (similar to the prohibitions of business on Tishah B'Av and of doing laundry during the week of Tishah B'Av[3]). The *Maharsha*'s contention is based on the fact that the *Beraisa* references the *pasuk*, "The teachings of Hashem are just…," only with regard to its latter ruling, namely, that we suspend the studies of children, but not in reference to its first ruling, that Torah study is forbidden. This implies that the prohibition of Torah study is due to a different cause, as stated. *Rashi*, however, states clearly that the reason for the first halachah is also because the *pasuk* states that Torah "gladdens the heart."

---

1   *Orach Chaim* 554:1.
2   *Taanis* 30a.
3   As stated by *Rashi* in *Taanis* 29a.

The Gemara records a dispute between the *Tanna Kama* and Rabbi Yehudah as to whether it is permissible for a person to study an area of Torah with which he is unfamiliar.[4] The *Tanna Kama* permits it but Rabbi Yehudah prohibits it. *Rashi* explains that the *Tanna Kama*'s reasoning is that when a person studies an unfamiliar topic, he is troubled by the toil necessary to understand it. It is therefore permissible to do so on Tishah B'Av.

Rashi does not, however, provide a reason for the position of Rabbi Yehudah (whose view we follow). The *Taz* suggests, that although study of an unfamiliar topic initially causes a person distress, he ultimately derives joy from it when he achieves clarity.[5] Therefore, the Chachamim forbade commencing the study of a new topic on account of the joy of concluding it. (He notes that Rabbi Yehudah's logic is consistent with his ruling in *Mo'ed Katan* 9b, that a woman may apply limestone to her face on Chol Hamoed, although it causes pain, because it ultimately brings her joy once she removes the lime and is left with improved skin. In both cases, the action is determined by its final result—whether to be stringent or lenient.)

According to the *Maharsha*, this form of study would be forbidden regardless of these arguments, for although it causes a person distress, it still serves to distract him from mourning. The *Taz* did not mention the *Maharsha*'s reason because he follows the view of the *Beis Yosef* and other *Poskim*, who hold like *Rashi* that the main reason for the prohibition is because Torah study brings joy.

The *Taz* raises an additional question: why is the Torah study of children suspended? It is well-known that children do not enjoy studying (hence the expression, "Like children running away from the house of study"[6]). Why then, should their Torah study be forbidden, given that it does not cause them joy? He answers that the prohibition was made on account of the enjoyment of the *melamed* (teacher).

---

4   *Taanis* ibid.
5   554:2.
6   *Midrash Aggadah*, cited in *Ramban* to *Bamidbar* 10:35.

The *Aruch Hashulchan* challenges this answer.[7] Teaching is generally burdensome for the *melamdim*, not a source of enjoyment. Surely this is not a basis to forbid the Torah study of children! He answers that although a *melamed* finds teaching bothersome, it grants internal pleasure to his Jewish soul, thus Chazal forbade it. This answer seems somewhat forced.

It would seem, rather, that Chazal did not wish to differentiate between cases, and thus forbade the study of any portion of Torah that causes joy. Therefore, it was still prohibited even in situations that would not bring a person joy, such as teaching young children, or studying a topic with which one is unfamiliar. In fact, if this were not the case, the entire decree would be utterly subjective, for who can decide who enjoys Torah study and who does not? Surely, it is dependent on the situation, the setting, and the time, as well as the style of study and the mood of the student! Therefore, Chazal did not make any differentiation, and only permitted the study of sections that discuss somber subjects, which cause sadness.

Is There a Mitzvah of Talmud Torah on Tishah B'Av?

There is a dispute among the Acharonim as to whether the mitzvah of *talmud Torah* applies on Tishah B'Av. The *Mateh Yehudah* states that although it is permissible to study somber subjects on Tishah B'Av, there is no obligation to study Torah as there usually is on every other day.[8] However, Rav Chaim Palagi rules that there is an obligation to study Torah on Tishah B'Av, and a person should fulfill it by studying the somber sections of Torah.[9] This was also the staunch opinion of my teacher, the Klausenberger Rebbe, *zt"l*, as stated in his *Teshuvos Divrei Yatziv*.[10] In his view, since it is permissible to study certain areas, there is an absolute obligation to study them, for there is no such concept as optional Torah study; if it is permissible, it is obligatory.

---

7   Ibid. 2.
8   *Orach Chaim* 554.
9   *Mo'ed L'Chol Chai* 10.
10 *Orach Chaim* 2, 240.

However, it is apparent from the Rishonim that there is no obligation of Torah study on Tishah B'Av. The *Ritva* asks how the Gemara can state that a mourner is obligated in all mitzvos except for tefillin—surely he is also forbidden from studying Torah?[11] He offers two answers: First, we cannot make inferences from a rule stated in the Gemara in this way. Second, a mourner is obligated to study Torah, but he discharges his obligation by reciting *k'rias Shema* in the morning and evening.

The *Ritva*'s words are puzzling, for he later states that a mourner may study somber topics since the halachos of a mourner are the same as those of Tishah B'Av.[12] Yet here he states that a mourner is either exempt from Torah study entirely or that he fulfills his obligation by reciting *k'rias Shema*! We see that in the view of the *Ritva*, a mourner does not have the same halachah as usual, and has no **obligation** to study Torah day and night, as on a regular day.

Elsewhere I have discussed the notion of exempting oneself of the obligation of Torah study by reciting *k'rias Shema*. I cite the position of the *Ritva* that in fact, a person cannot exempt himself by reciting *Shema*; the Gemara's intent is that he is not obligated to study this particular chapter.[13] (He initially suggests a different explanation—that a person can discharge his obligation by reciting *Shema* in a case of great need. He then states that the primary view is that a person can never thereby fulfill his requirement to study Torah.) In this light we must conclude that Tishah B'Av is indeed different from a regular day in this regard.

In fact, this question is already addressed by *Rashi*, who states: "The statement that a mourner is obligated in all the mitzvos in the Torah except for tefillin [did not include Torah study], because that [statement] was only made with regard to other general mitzvos, but these [carry an exemption for a different reason, namely, because] they carry an aspect of joy."[14] *Rashi* was troubled as to why it is not stated that a mourner is exempt from Torah study, and he answers that a mourner is indeed

---

11 *Mo'ed Katan* 15a.
12 Ibid. 21a, 23a.
13 *Nedarim* 8a.
14 *Mo'ed Katan* 21a, s.v. "*V'assur li'kros*."

exempt from Torah study because it gladdens the heart, whereas the exemption from tefillin is derived from a *pasuk*. Clearly, *Rashi* also maintains that a mourner is exempt from Torah study.

This assertation cannot be rejected by suggesting that according to *Rashi*, a mourner may not even study somber topics—which is the view of *Tosafos*[15]—for *Rashi* clearly states that a mourner is exempt from Torah study due to the aspect of joy, not due to the Torah derivation from the *pasuk*, "Keep silent from your cries."[16] It is therefore logical to apply the position stated by *Tosafos*, that a mourner has the same halachos as Tishah B'Av and the same parameters apply to both; thus there is no prohibition of studying somber topics.

A further source is the *Shibbolei Haleket*, who rules that on Tishah B'Av and during the mourning period, a person should not recite *birchas haTorah*.[17] Clearly, he maintains that there is no obligation to study Torah, even though the *Beraisa* explicitly states it is permissible to study the somber portions of Torah.

In fact, we may reason that even those who do hold that we recite *birchas haTorah* do not necessarily maintain that a person is **obligated** in Torah study. Since a person will be reciting *pesukim* in *k'rias Shema* and *tefillah* regardless, he requires *birchas haTorah* for that even if he has no further obligation to study Torah. This is akin to the ruling of the *Shulchan Aruch* that women recite *birchas haTorah*.[18] (It is apparent that the *Shibbolei Haleket* does not require *birchas haTorah* to be recited before *k'rias Shema*—I have elaborated on this topic elsewhere.)

We should also mention the *Kli Yakar*'s comments in *Parashas Toldos*, on the *pasuk*, "And Eisav hated Yaakov on account of the berachah with which his father had blessed him, and Eisav said in his heart, 'Let the days of mourning for my father come near, and I shall kill Yaakov my brother.'"[19] The *Kli Yakar* explains Eisav's plan. Since a mourner is forbidden from studying Torah, Yaakov would not have the merit of Torah

---

15   Ibid. s.v. *"V'assur."*
16   *Yechezkel* 24:17.
17   *Hilchos Semachos* 26, citing a *Teshuvas Geonim*.
18   *Orach Chaim* 47:14.
19   *Bereishis* 27:41.

to protect himself during those days, and Eisav would be successful in killing him. But if a mourner is indeed obligated in Torah study as usual, why would the merit of the Torah not protect him? It would be far-fetched to suggest that Torah study without joy would not offer protection. Clearly, the *Kli Yakar* assumes that a mourner is not **obligated** in Torah study.

It therefore emerges that although a mourner may study somber topics, he is not bound by the obligation to study Torah.

If so, the question arises; since he is permitted to study, why should he not be obligated to do so?

We may offer several approaches:

1. Above we cited the view of the *Aruch Hashulchan*, that even if a person does not experience the pleasure of Torah, there is nevertheless an inherent joy in its study. For this reason, children's studies are suspended, though they do not enjoy them. If so, it is possible that even when it comes to the somber sections of Torah, there is a certain innate joy in their study. In fact, it is characteristic of Torah study that even while studying somber topics, a person can develop novel ideas of Torah and *mussar*, which gladden his heart. Nevertheless, Chazal permitted the study of these sections because of their somber tone; however, they did not obligate a person to study them, since they also cause joy.

(According to this approach, it would seem to be preferable to focus on the mourning rather than study the somber topics, which is based on a leniency. However, today, when we do not mourn the *churban* sufficiently, it would appear to be a mitzvah to study the portions of rebuke found in the *Neviim*, and the *Aggados* of Chazal regarding the *churban*—for only thereby will we instill some feeling in our hearts for the *churban*.)

2. We have explained elsewhere that fundamentally, the obligation of Torah study applies when a person is free of other activities.[20] Granted, when a person is in mourning, he is not considered to be engaged in

---

20 As stated by the *Ohr Sameach* at the beginning of *Hilchos Talmud Torah*; *Kovetz He'aros*, *Yevamos* 62; *Kehillos Yaakov*, *Shabbos* 11.

a mitzvah that would exempt him from Torah study, for if that would be the case, he should be exempt from all mitzvos (which is not the case). Nevertheless, mourning is no less than any other of his basic needs, which exempt him from Torah study during his involvement with them (I have elaborated on this concept elsewhere). If so, it is possible that on Tishah B'Av, since a person is engaged in mourning at the behest of Chazal, he is exempt from Torah study since mourning is no different than being involved with his personal needs. (This is despite the fact that studying somber topics is not a contradiction to mourning.) According to this approach, a person who is not "engrossed in mourning" would have an obligation to study Torah.

3. The best approach appears to be the following. The primary fulfillment of Torah study is achieved by learning a topic that one's heart desires and delighting in the study of Torah. Hashem granted every Jew his own portion in Torah and planted within each of them the disposition and intellect to cleave to Hashem through a particular area of Torah, as stated by the *Maharsha*[21] and the *Maalas HaTorah* by the brother of the *Vilna Gaon*. The main path of Torah study is accompanied by joy, as stated by the *Taz*, who explains that the rule "Mitzvos were not given to derive pleasure from" does not apply to Torah study, for the **primary mitzvah is to enjoy the study of Torah**.[22] This principle is also stated by Rabbeinu Avraham Min HaHar.[23] We will cite his wonderful comments in their entirety:

> *Some ask: Why is it forbidden to study sefarim [belonging to a person who has vowed not to benefit from them]? Surely, Torah study is a mitzvah, and "mitzvos were not given to derive pleasure therefrom"!*
>
> *This is not a question, for the rule that "mitzvos were not given to derive pleasure therefrom" only applies to a mitzvah that pertains to an action. When a person performs [a mitzvah of*

---

21 *Sanhedrin* 91b, s.v. "*Kol Hamonei'a.*"
22 *Yoreh Deah* 221:43.
23 *Nedarim* 48a.

that sort], he does not intend to derive benefit; he performs it not for his own benefit but to fulfill the commandment of Hashem. The mitzvah of Torah study, however, which is a contemplation of the heart and knowledge of the truth—**the primary obligation is to envision the truth and derive pleasure and enjoyment from knowledge, to gladden his heart and mind, as it states, "The teachings of Hashem are just, they gladden the heart."** A mourner is therefore prohibited from reading Neviim and Kesuvim because they gladden his heart involuntarily. Therefore, it is not appropriate to apply to Torah [the rule] that mitzvos were not given to derive pleasure therefrom, **for the main mitzvah is the joy and pleasure in what a person attains and understands of his study."**

It therefore appears that when a person is only permitted to study somber sections of Torah that cause him sadness, it is not possible for him to be **obligated** in Torah study.

In spite of this, it seems obvious that a person fulfills the mitzvah of *talmud Torah* if he does study on Tishah B'Av; the only dispute is to whether he is obligated to do so. In this light, we can contest the proof that my dear brother Rabbi Chaim brought from the ruling of the *Shulchan Aruch*, that a person going to visit his *rebbi* may pass through a body of water until even his neck is submerged—which amounts to washing oneself (on Tishah B'Av).[24] The *Mishnah Berurah* states that although there is only a mitzvah for a person to visit his *rebbi* on Yom Tov, it is still considered a mitzvah on Tishah B'Av, as he may hear some words of Torah from him.[25] If it were true that there is no obligation to study Torah on Tishah B'Av, how is it permitted for a person to enter a body of water in order to hear words of Torah from his *rebbi*? We must say that there is an obligation to study the somber topics.

However, in light of our contention above we may say that the prohibition of bathing was waived not only for the fulfillment of an

---

24   *Orach Chaim* 554:12.
25   Ibid. 23.

obligation, but also for the fulfillment of a non-compulsory mitzvah, like visiting one's *rebbi*. (This is also the implication of the *Shulchan Aruch* who states, "Or for any mitzvah-related matter.") If so, it is certainly the case that the student will fulfill a mitzvah by visiting his *rebbi* on Tishah B'Av as well, since he will hear words of Torah relating to the fast day or other permissible topics.

It is also possible that the case of the *Shulchan Aruch* is of a person going to visit his *rebbi* on Tishah B'Av, but who will remain with him until the day's conclusion, when he will then hear words of Torah from him.

Reciting K'rias Shema When Putting on Tefillin

There is a dispute among the *Poskim* as to whether one should recite *k'rias Shema* when he dons tefillin on Tishah B'Av afternoon. The *Mishnah Berurah*'s ruling is that a person should wear tefillin but not recite *Shema*.[26] However, many have the practice to recite *Shema* even while wearing the tefillin of Rabbeinu Tam.[27] The *Shevus Yaakov* offers a *chiddush* that a person may daven *Maariv* early while it is still day, while wearing tefillin, so that he may recite *Shema* wearing tefillin—and should then remove them before the *Amidah*.[28] His position is cited by the *Shaarei Teshuvah*, who disagrees, arguing that it makes little difference whether a person recites *Shema* during *Maariv*, or if he lays tefillin, recites *Shema*, and davens *Maariv* later in its appropriate time.[29] The *Shaar Hatziyun* questions this assumption, for it would surely be forbidden to recite *Shema* prior to *Maariv* as it is considered Torah study.[30] Therefore, it would seem to be better to daven *Maariv* early in order to recite *k'rias Shema* while wearing tefillin.

This comment of the *Shaar Hatziyun* seems puzzling, for even if a person would daven *Maariv* while it is still day, he would not fulfill the mitzvah of *k'rias Shema*; rather, since it is before its appropriate time;

---

26 555:5.
27 See *Kaf Hachaim* 555:7 and 554:19.
28 2, 24.
29 555.
30 Ibid. 4.

he would be considered to be studying Torah. If so, what difference is there between reciting *Shema* during *Maariv* or beforehand?

However, we may certainly argue that reciting *k'rias Shema* as part of the order of *tefillah* constitutes *tefillah*—which is permitted on Tishah B'Av—and not Torah study. Its halachah is similar to that of other passages relating to the order of the day, such as *Parashas HaTamid and Eizehu Mekoman*, which may be recited. In fact, there is an even greater reason to permit the recital of *k'rias Shema* than the recital of the other passages, for once Chazal instituted that *k'rias Shema* and its berachos be juxtaposed to the *Amidah* so as to begin the *tefillah* having just uttered words of Torah,[31] they are considered part of the prayer service.

K'rias Shema during *Shacharis* has the status of *tefillah* with regard to other halachos as well. The *Shulchan Aruch* rules that *k'rias Shema* and its berachos can be recited until the fourth hour, even though the mitzvah of *k'rias Shema* can only be fulfilled until the third hour, **for it is considered part of tefillah.**[32] By contrast, after the fourth hour it can only be recited without its berachos, for it is only like reciting Torah. (The *Levush* states that until the fourth hour, it is still considered to be "within its time" to a degree—which is very surprising.)[33]

A further proof can be brought from the *Yerushalmi*, which states that a person can only fulfill his requirement of *birchas haTorah* with the berachah of *Ahavah Rabbah* if he studies Torah immediately afterward, although he has already recited *Shema*. The *Beis Yosef* explains that this is because this recitation of *Shema* is like *tefillah*, thus a person must study Torah immediately afterward to discharge his obligation of *birchas haTorah*.[34]

In addition, this is clearly the intent of the *Ramban*, who rules that it is permissible to recite *Eizehu Mekoman* and the passages that discuss the order of the day, proving it from the fact that we recite *k'rias Shema* with its berachos.[35] This seems puzzling—surely *k'rias Shema* is different

---

31 *Yerushalmi, Berachos* 1:1; *Tosafos, Berachos* 2a.
32 *Orach Chaim* 58:6.
33 Ibid.
34 Ibid. 47.
35 Cited by the *Tur, Orach Chaim* 554.

since it is a *mitzvah d'Oraisa*, and a Rabbinic decree not to study Torah on Tishah B'Av surely cannot override a positive Torah mitzvah! (I have seen that some Acharonim maintain that Chazal indeed waived the mitzvah of Torah study, as they have the authority to passively override a Torah mitzvah. However, I have explained in *Minchas Asher* that Chazal only have this power when their intent is to distance a person from sinning, but not in any other context.[36]) Rather, it seems clear that the *Ramban* is referring to *k'rias Shema* recited during the fourth hour. Although a person does not thereby fulfill the mitzvah of *k'rias Shema*, it is nonetheless part of the order of *tefillah*, and Chazal never made their decree in that regard. It is therefore logical that the *Ramban* is able to draw a comparison from "*k'rias Shema* with its berachos"—for since it was inserted into the order of *tefillah*, it has the status of *tefillah* and not Torah study. Thus, the same may likewise apply to all other passages related to the order of *tefillah*.

Therefore, the most plausible view seems to be that of the *Shevus Yaakov* and *Shaar Hatziyun*, that a person may daven *Maariv* while it is still day and recite *Shema*, even if it is forbidden to recite *Shema* specifically for the mitzvah of tefillin.

When Torah Thoughts Enter One's Mind

The Acharonim discuss whether a person whose soul is bound up with Torah study, for whom Torah thoughts enter his mind unwittingly, may write these thoughts down on Tishah B'Av. The *Shaarei Teshuvah* rules that he may not, for it would bring him joy.[37] However, the *S'dei Chemed*[38] and the *Kaf Hachaim*[39] both cite several Acharonim who are lenient. The *S'dei Chemed* concludes that a person may write down a summary so as not to forget his thoughts, and then write them in detail after Tishah B'Av.

The basis of their dispute needs examination. Seemingly, they are discussing *chiddushim* pertaining to topics that may be studied on

---

36   *Pesachim* 79, 1.
37   554:13.
38   *Maareches Bein Hametzarim* 2:10.
39   554:10.

Tishah B'Av, for how could it be permissible to write aspects of Torah about which one is forbidden even to think? However, I saw that Rav Shlomo Kluger states in *Chochmas Shlomo* that although a person may not intentionally sit and learn on Tishah B'Av, if thoughts of Torah occur to him momentarily, he has not violated any prohibition and he is not required to push them away.[40] (It seems that this only applies to studying Torah on Tishah B'Av, and not to entertaining thoughts of Torah in a soiled area, which was only permitted if he cannot control the thought from entering his mind.)[41] It is therefore possible that just as it is permissible to temporarily think about Torah, it is also permissible to write down these thoughts. Although a distinction can be made between thinking and writing, nevertheless, Rav Kluger's comparison is not unreasonable. It is further possible that although it is forbidden to develop and create Torah thoughts, a person is not required to lose that which he has already attained—for Chazal state, "Whoever forgets a single matter of his studies, the Torah considers it as if he is deserving of death!"[42] It is therefore permissible to write one's thoughts down so as not to forget them.

One Who Longs to Study Torah on Tishah B'Av

The biographers of the Rogatchover Gaon relate that while he was mourning, he studied Torah as usual. I myself heard from my dear son-in-law Rav Binyamin Beinish that his illustrious grandfather, Rav Avrohom Binyomin Zilberberg, the *av beis din* of Saint Petersburg, accompanied his grandfather Rav Naftali of Viyereshov to visit the Rogatchover Gaon while he was sitting *shivah*, and they saw him studying Torah. When they asked him about it, the Gaon replied that Chazal indeed forbade Torah study, but they did not require a person to give up his life over this prohibition.

I heard that one of the Gedolei Ha'dor was very surprised by this, for what good is there in Torah study when it is in violation of an *aveirah*?

---

40   Ibid.
41   As stated in *Zevachim* 102b. See *Minchas Asher, Devarim* 43.
42   *Avos* 3:8.

Surely this gives no pleasure to the Giver of the Torah. However, this is not problematic at all, as there is a support for this concept from both the *Bavli* and *Yerushalmi*.

The Gemara states,

> *Rava said, we learned this halachah from Rabbi Elazar bar Rabbi Shimon, who stated in the bathroom...but how could he have done so—surely Rabbah bar bar Chanah stated in the name of Rabbi Yochanan that a person is permitted to think about Torah in any place except for a bathhouse and a bathroom? [The Gemara answers,] A case of duress is different.*[43]

Rashi comments, "Duress is different—for his teaching was so frequently in his mouth, and he would think about it against his will. I have heard a similar concept in *Maseches Kiddushin* (33a)."

We see that even regarding the prohibition of thinking about Torah in the bathroom—which is more stringent than that of studying Torah on Tishah B'Av and while mourning—a person who is under duress because his learning is constantly on his lips has no prohibition. This would be all the more true in our case.

Additionally, the *Yerushalmi* states that a mourner who pines for Torah study may learn Torah during his mourning period.[44]

Obviously, the great Rogatchover Gaon pined for Torah and studied Torah almost against his will, which carries no prohibition, as stated. However, it is clear that this should not be relied on as practical halachah; it was only said with regard to the greatest Gedolim, such as the Rogatchover.

With that said, the Gemara in *Zevachim* seems problematic. Although Rabbi Elazar bar Rabbi Shimon could not stop himself contemplating thoughts of Torah, as *Rashi* states, why was it permitted for him to verbalize them? It is clear that he spoke them out loud because Rava

---

43 *Zevachim* 102b.
44 *Mo'ed Katan* 3:5. However, the *Beis Yosef* states, "It is furthermore stated in the *Yerushalmi* that a person who pines for Torah may study, but this is not cited by the *Poskim*" (*Yoreh Deah* 384).

testified that Rabbi Elazar bar Rabbi Shimon stated these words in the bathroom, which means they must have been audible to others!

We are forced to say one of two things:

- The Tanna was in a state of duress not only with regard to thinking about Torah, but also with regard to verbalizing his thoughts. This would be the intent of *Rashi*'s statement, "For his teaching was so frequently **in his mouth**, and **he would think about it** against his will," which alludes to two separate points. This could be understood in two ways: (1) The Tanna was in a state of duress with regard to disseminating Torah and teaching wisdom to his students, as per Chazal's emphasis on the importance of teaching Torah to one's students. (2) This is the manner of Torah study, namely, to verbalize one's learning and not to merely think about it, as stated in *Maseches Eiruvin*: "They are a source of life to those who express them by mouth,"[45] as expounded by Beruriah, the wife of Rabbi Meir.

- Since it is also forbidden to think about Torah in the bathroom, there is no additional prohibition in speaking; therefore, since he was under duress with regard to thinking, it was also permissible for him to verbalize his thoughts.

The Gemara also relates that Rabbi Shimon bar Rebbi did not stand up before Rav Chiya in the bathroom and Rabbi Chiya was bothered by it.[46] They suggested to Rav Chiya that Rabbi Shimon was possibly thinking about Torah and did not notice that Rav Chiya had passed him by. Though it is forbidden to think about Torah in a bathhouse, a case of duress is different, as explained above.

The Gemara only states, "Perhaps he was thinking about Torah," which certainly does not imply that they heard him studying Torah out loud. Like in *Zevachim*, *Rashi* comments, "His teaching was so frequently in his mouth," which implies that this expression does not necessarily refer to verbalizing Torah, but to the fact that Torah was in

---

45   54a.
46   *Kiddushin* 33a.

his mouth and heart, and he was therefore under duress with regard to thinking about it.

Rashi states in *Zevachim*, "I have heard a similar concept in *Maseches Kiddushin*." I do not understand his intent with this reference, for the matter is seemingly as explicit in *Kiddushin* as it is in *Zevachim*—I have not seen any additional points in *Kiddushin* over *Zevachim*.

FOUR

Torah Study When Tishah B'Av or Erev Tishah B'Av Falls on Shabbos

The *Shulchan Aruch* rules: "If Tishah B'Av occurs on Sunday, or if it occurs on Shabbos and is postponed until after Shabbos, [a person may] eat meat and drink wine during the *seudah ha'mafsekes*, and set his table even [with a meal] like the feast of Shlomo during his reign."[1] The basis for this ruling is the Gemara in *Maseches Eiruvin*.[2]

The *Mishnah Berurah* cites the *Magen Avraham* who rules that a person should nonetheless eat in a state of sorrow and not sit among friends.[3] He then cites the opposing view of the *Bechor Shor* who rules that a person who sits among friends every Shabbos and refrains from doing so specifically when Tishah B'Av falls on Shabbos has violated the prohibition of a public display of mourning on Shabbos.

---

1 *Orach Chaim* 552:10.
2 41a.
3 552:23.

The implication of the *Bechor Shor* is that this leniency is only given to a person for whom this is his regular behavior. However, the *Igros Moshe* rules that even a person who does not normally behave in this way may do so on this Shabbos, for we do not find that eating meat and drinking wine is only permitted for a person who is accustomed to it.[4] In Rav Moshe's view, there does not seem to be a difference between the prohibition to consume meat and wine, and to sit among friends.

The view of the *Bechor Shor* and *Mishnah Berurah* appears to be that the issue of consuming meat and wine is indeed different, for Chazal permitted their consumption, as stated by the Gemara. Therefore, given that this is the manner of *kavod* and *oneg* of the Shabbos *seudos*, unrestricted permission was given. However, when it comes to other prohibitions for which Chazal did not give a leniency, the matter is purely dependent on whether each individual case would constitute a public display of mourning or not.

Four Opinions

The *Rama* states, "It is customary not to study [Torah] on Erev Tishah B'Av from midday onward—other than the subjects that may be studied on Tishah B'Av. Therefore, if it coincides with Shabbos, we do not recite *Pirkei Avos*."[5]

There is a four-way dispute among the *Poskim* with regard to the halachah of studying Torah on Erev Tishah B'Av that coincides with Shabbos:

1. The *Maharil* and *Rama* maintain that Shabbos has the same law as weekdays, therefore, just as it is customary not to study Torah on Erev Tishah B'Av after midday during the week, the same applies on Shabbos.
2. The *Maharshal*, *Vilna Gaon*, and *Maamar Mordechai* maintain that it is permissible even during the week, and that this custom is an excessive stringency that causes *bittul Torah*.

---

4 *Orach Chaim* 4, 112:1.
5 Ibid. 553:2.

3. The view of the *Taz*[6] and *Maharam MiLublin*[7] is that although during the week, a person should indeed not study subjects that will bring him joy, there is no need to be stringent on Shabbos, for a person may lay his table with a meal akin to the feast of Shlomo HaMelech, and it would not be logical to be stringent only with regard to Torah. This is also the view of Rav Yaakov Emden, as stated in *Mor U'Ketziah*[8] and *Siddur Beis Yaakov*, which is consistent with his ruling[9] that a person may not read something that will cause him sadness on Shabbos. He adds that studying somber topics on Shabbos involves a possible transgression, for the fact that on every other Shabbos he studies *Pirkei Avos* and this week studies somber topics may be considered a public display of mourning.
4. The *Magen Avraham* states a *chiddush* that when Tishah B'Av coincides with Shabbos, it may be forbidden to study Torah the entire day.[10] This view is already stated by the *Leket Yosher*.

The *Chasam Sofer* asserts that the custom not to learn on Erev Tishah B'Av is not due to mourning, but because the effect of Torah study is that a person delights in it long after he has finished learning, and his thoughts are constantly occupied with it.[11] As such, there is a concern that a person's mind will be focused on what he has studied that afternoon, even after sundown. According to this view, there would be no issue of making a public display of mourning because the prohibition of studying Torah has nothing to do with mourning but is due to the concern that the Torah will continue to give a person joy even after the conclusion of Shabbos.[12]

---

6   Ibid.
7   *Teshuvos* 91.
8   *Orach Chaim* 553.
9   *Mor U'Ketziah, Orach Chaim* 307.
10 553:7.
11 *Orach Chaim* 156.
12 See further, the additions of his son, the *Kesav Sofer, Teshuvos, Orach Chaim* 101.

When Tishah B'Av Is Postponed

The view of the *Magen Avraham*, that when Tishah B'Av coincides with Shabbos, it is forbidden to learn the entire day, is disputed by most *Poskim*, who only discuss a possible prohibition from midday onward. This dispute seems to depend upon a fundamental question as to the very essence of Tishah B'Av that coincides with Shabbos and which is postponed to Sunday: Is **the day itself** postponed—as if the tenth of Av was actually Tishah B'Av—and Shabbos carries no aspect of the fast day? Or is it the **laws of the day**, such as fasting and public mourning, that are postponed because they cannot be practiced on Shabbos, but anything that does not contravene the sanctity of Shabbos remains in place? If the essence of the day itself is postponed, there would clearly be no prohibition in studying Torah on Shabbos morning, for it is like any other day. The prohibition would thus only begin at midday. However, if it is only the halachos that are postponed, the view of the *Magen Avraham* would seem logical. Given that there are topics that may be studied, it would be forbidden to study subjects that cause joy throughout the day.

This point appears to be the subject of dispute between the *Shulchan Aruch* and the *Rama*. The *Shulchan Aruch* rules, "If Tishah B'Av coincides with Shabbos, all [the five afflictions] are permitted—even marital relations."[13] The *Rama* comments, "There are those who forbid marital relations—and that is our practice." Thus, according to the *Shulchan Aruch*, there is no element of Tishah B'Av at all, and even private mourning—which does apply on Shabbos—is not practiced on this Shabbos. The *Rama*, however, maintains that the day itself is not postponed—only specific halachos.

Elsewhere, I have discussed the question of the *Minchas Chinuch*, who asks why the four fast days are postponed when they coincide with Shabbos.[14] Surely, the mitzvos of *kavod* and *oneg* on Shabbos are *divrei kabbalah* (institutions of the Neviim)—"And you shall proclaim Shabbos as a [day of] delight; and the sanctified [day] of Hashem, a [day

---

13 *Orach Chaim* 554:19.
14 Mitzvah 301.

of] honor"[15]—as are the four fasts.[16] This being so, it would surely be preferable to be passive—to sit alone and fast, and transgress the mitzvah of *oneg Shabbos* passively—rather than to eat, and actively violate the fasts!

I wrote that this can be explained from two angles: (1) although the mitzvah of *oneg Shabbos* is *divrei kabbalah*, there is a Torah prohibition of fasting due to the mitzvah of *lechem mishneh*, or due to it being a *mikra kodesh*, and (2) Shabbos itself is *min haTorah*, which is not the case with regard to the other fasts. I elaborated elsewhere on these points, but regardless, the fact that none of the Rishonim raise this seemingly simple question indicates that it fundamentally does not exist. (I frequently say that strong and challenging questions necessarily have very simple answers.)

It therefore appears that the Neviim instituted from the outset that when a fast coincides with Shabbos, it is postponed until after Shabbos. Shabbos was fixed in place at the beginning of time, but the fasts may be observed on a different day. The Neviim themselves decreed both the institution of the fast and its postponement until after Shabbos. (Nonetheless, a fast that has been postponed remains more lenient, because it is not the primary day of the fast or the day on which the tragedies occurred.)

However, this is not the view of the *Minchas Chinuch*. He states a *chiddush* that the specific day of the fast does not have the status of *divrei kabbalah* (i.e. from the Neviim), but of *divrei sofrim* (i.e. from the *Rabbanan*) The Neviim only instituted the **months** of the fasts, as the *pasuk* states, "The fast of **the fourth** [month], the fast of **the fifth** [month], the fast of **the seventh** [month], and the fast of **the tenth** [month]." Therefore, the **day of the fast**—which is *divrei sofrim*, defers to Shabbos, which is *divrei kabbalah*.

It would seem that the dispute between the *Shulchan Aruch* and the *Rama* depends on these two approaches. According to the *Minchas Chinuch*, we view this case as we do every contradiction between two

---

15   Yeshayahu 58:13.
16   Zechariah 8:19.

mitzvos and obligations. It is therefore possible that only the laws of Tishah B'Av that are in contravention of Shabbos are postponed, but the ninth day of Av always retains the status and halachos of Tishah B'Av. Following our approach, however, it is clear that Shabbos does not have the status of Tishah B'Av at all, since it was initially instituted to be postponed to the tenth of Av, as stated.

It is possible that the ruling of the *Beis Yosef* is thereby consistent with his view elsewhere. In *siman* 550, he cites the *Avudraham* that the tenth of Teves that coincides with Shabbos is not postponed, for it states, "On this very day."[17] The *Beis Yosef* rejects this, however, and states that he does not know the basis for this.[18] The *Griz* in *Hilchos Taanis* explains the *Avudraham* based on the approach of the *Minchas Chinuch*, namely, that in reality, all of the fasts would override Shabbos were it not to be possible on account of the *takanas Neviim* to postpone them to a different day. Since they did not institute a specific day, the fasts may be postponed, hence, *divrei sofrim* (fasting on a specific day) is set aside in the face of *divrei kabbalah* (*oneg Shabbos*). However, the Neviim did institute a specific day for the tenth of Teves, and it can therefore justifiably override *oneg Shabbos* in a passive fashion.

It appears that the *Beis Yosef*, consistent with his view as explained above, maintains that all the fasts were instituted by the Neviim on a specific day, but they nevertheless decreed that the fasts should be postponed if they coincide with Shabbos. For this reason, he disagrees with the *Avudraham*.[19]

The *Rama*, however, appears to contradict himself, for in *siman* 554,[20] he rules that when Tishah B'Av coincides with Shabbos, marital relations are forbidden, and mourning is observed privately. However, in *siman* 553,[21] he rules that Torah study is permissible, and the custom prohibiting it only begins from midday. Clearly, then, there is no

---

17 *Yechezkel* 24:2.
18 See *Ohr Sameach, Hilchos Taanis,* chap. 5, who provides an astounding source for the *Avudraham* from *Eiruvin* 40b.
19 See *Minchas Asher, Mo'adim* 2, 43, where we have elaborated on the topic of the tenth of Teves.
20 19.
21 2.

imperative to suggest that these halachos are interconnected and since the main aspects of mourning do not apply on Shabbos, Torah study was not prohibited at all. This is especially apparent seeing as a person may lay his table with a meal like the feast of Shlomo HaMelech—as argued by the *Taz* and those who support his view.

A Source for the Minchas Chinuch

It has been suggested that a basis for the position of *Minchas Chinuch*—that the Neviim only instituted the months of the fasts, but not the specific days—can be found in the *Tashbetz*.[22] However, in my opinion, although the *Tashbetz* does provide support for the basic premise of the *Minchas Chinuch*, they are two distinct views that are not connected. To explain this, I will quote the text of the *Tashbetz*:

> *The Neviim who instituted the fast of the fourth month did not tie it exclusively to one day. Rather,* **they left it to beis din to alter the day, connecting it to similar tragedies**. *And that is the [day of] the breaching [of the wall]—whether it would be on the ninth or on any other day—provided that it is in the right month, it is handed over to beis din to decide on the day [commemorating] the breaching [of the wall].*

In my opinion, it is clear that the *Tashbetz* never entertained the thought that the Neviim only decreed a month during which anyone can decide which day they want to observe the fast. The Neviim certainly instituted a day for the fast, but they gave the Sages of future generations the allowance to adjust the day and connect it to similar tragedies. For example, the day on which the wall of the First Beis Hamikdash was breached was the ninth of Tammuz, but the wall of the Second Beis Hamikdash was breached on the seventeenth. The Neviim did not insist that the original fast remain on the ninth of Tammuz; they gave permission for future generations to alter it to the seventeenth. However, it is clear that there always needs to be one day on which the entire nation would fast—based on the decision of the Sages.

---

22   2, 271.

Two Aspects to the Day

Elsewhere, I have discussed the position of the *Griz* and *Minchas Chinuch* that there are two aspects to the prohibition of washing on Tishah B'Av.[23] From a perspective of *aveilus*, it would only be forbidden to wash with hot water, as stated in *Yoreh De'ah* with regard to a mourner who may wash his face, hands, and feet with cold water.[24] The prohibition stated by the *Shulchan Aruch* that on Tishah B'Av a person may not even dip his finger in water, is an additional stringency due to the comparison between Tishah B'Av and Yom Kippur.[25]

In light of their view, I explained the ruling of the *Mishnah Berurah* that according to the *Rama*, who forbids marital relations on Tishah B'Av that coincides with Shabbos, it would also be forbidden for a person to wash his hands with hot water.[26] This seems puzzling. Why does he only state that it would be forbidden to wash with hot water? Surely, on Tishah B'Av it is forbidden to wash even with cold water, and even to dip one's finger in water! Rather, the opinion that private mourning is observed on Shabbos agrees that this is limited to the halachos of mourning. However, the added stringencies of the fast that are due to its comparison with Yom Kippur would not apply on Shabbos, for if a person is permitted to set a feast like that of Shlomo HaMelech, there is clearly no element of Yom Kippur.

However, as I wrote there, in my opinion there are not two separate elements to the prohibition. Rather, it is as per the simple understanding of the Gemara in *Maseches Taanis*, "Everything that is forbidden for a mourner, is forbidden on Tishah B'Av."[27] The Gemara states that this is the basis for the prohibition of washing, anointing oneself, etc., on Tishah B'Av.

With regard to the question that if the halachos of Tishah B'Av are synonymous with those of a mourner, why is it even prohibited to dip

---

23 *Minchas Asher, Mo'adim* 2, 43.
24 381:1.
25 *Orach Chaim* 554:7.
26 554:39.
27 30a.

one's finger in water—a halachah that does not apply to a mourner? This question is raised by the *Ritva*, who answers that a leniency was made for a mourner, since the restrictions last for seven days, whereas with regard to Tishah B'Av, which is one day, Chazal were more stringent.[28] (In truth, it seems clear that if the intent of the *Mishnah Berurah* was in line with the *Griz* and *Minchas Chinuch* as explained above, he would not have left his words vague; rather, he would have elaborated in the *Biur Halachah* and *Shaar Hatziyun*, as he does in all such cases.)

The *Mishnah Berurah*'s intent clearly seems to be that there cannot be any prohibition of washing one's hands with cold water, for a person washes his hands for the Shabbos *seudah*—both at the beginning and end of the meal. Clearly, this is not merely a suspended prohibition, but one that is waived entirely. Thus, since a person may eat and drink, no prohibition was made with regard to washing with cold water. However, there is still room to examine the matter, for there is still a prohibition to wash with hot water.

---

28 *Taanis* 13b.

Sichos

FIVE

As If They Had Destroyed It

> *The fast of the fourth [month] and the fast of the fifth [month], the fast of the seventh [month] and the fast of the tenth [month], will become for the Jewish People [times of] gladness and joy and days of festivity, and truth and peace shall you love.*
>
> Zechariah 8:19

This *pasuk* is very puzzling. It begins with prayer, hope, and promise of a shining future, in which the days of fasting and mourning will become days of joy and light. How is this linked to the end of the *pasuk*, which contains words of admonition and rebuke, "truth and peace shall you love"?

I saw that the *Radak* and *Metzudos* explain that the promise of the beginning of the *pasuk* is conditional upon truth and peace being beloved. This matter requires explanation.

Chazal make the following statement: "Any generation in which [the Beis Hamikdash] is not built, is considered to have destroyed it."[1] These words are extremely piercing.

---

1   *Yerushalmi, Yoma* 5a.

It is considered that they destroyed it! Were we to be worthy of the Divine presence, we would immediately merit the Beis Hamikdash of fire descending from the Heavens.[2] And if we have not merited this, it is only because we were found unworthy, and it is therefore as if we have destroyed the Beis Hamikdash in our time.

During these difficult times, it is the duty of each individual to imagine and picture in his mind's eye the flames devouring the beams of the Beis Hamikdash, and the young Kohanim throwing the keys of the Sanctuary to the Heavens before jumping into the flames.

This places a heavy responsibility on every generation, every community, and every individual to consider his actions, to better his ways, and to do all he can to ensure the speedy rebuilding of the Beis Hamikdash.

Primarily, we need to strengthen ourselves in those areas that brought about the destruction of the First and Second *Batei Mikdash*, because those are the causes that prevent it being rebuilt in every generation. We must therefore consider why this great wrath was aroused and what caused the first and second *churban*? Let us examine the matter.

For What Was the Land Destroyed?

Chazal relate: "For what reason was the land destroyed? This was asked to the Sages, to the prophets, and to the angels, and they could not answer, until Hakadosh Baruch Hu Himself explained, 'For they forsook My Torah'—in that they didn't make a berachah on Torah first."[3] The *Ran* comments that the Beis Hamikdash was clearly not destroyed just because they did not recite *birchas haTorah*. Rather it was because "the Torah was not important in their eyes," and they did not study it for its own sake. It is not enough for us to engage in Torah study; the Torah has to be **important** to us. We must understand that "it is your life and the length of your days."[4] We must be aware that "a student who is exiled to a city of refuge, his *rebbi* is exiled with him, for the *pasuk* says, 'And he shall flee to one of these cities and live' (*Devarim* 4:42)—provide

---

2   Rashi and *Tosafos*, *Rosh Hashanah* 30, *Sukkah* 41, and *Shevuos* 15.
3   *Nedarim* 81a.
4   *Devarim* 30:20.

for him the means to live."⁵ The golden words of the *Rambam* must be fluent to us in our mouths and engraved on our hearts, "The lives of the masters and seekers of wisdom are considered like death without [Torah] study."⁶ We will not be worthy of the Divine presence until we rejoice in the words of Torah and revel in them, and realize that "they are our life and the lengthening of our days."

The *Degel Machaneh Ephraim* quotes his grandfather and teacher, the Baal Shem Tov, who stated that at the time of the *churban*, they did not say the blessing of "*V'haarev na*."⁷ He writes that he finds this perplexing, and it does indeed seem perplexing, for the third and final berachah—"*Asher bachar banu*"—is considered the superlative berachah;⁸ the first berachah is the *birkas ha'mitzvah* of "*Asher kideshanu b'mitzvosav*"; and "*V'haarev na*" is the least of the berachos—merely "*semuchah l'chaverta*—adjacent to its neighbor." If so, why did the Baal Shem Tov conclude that on account of **this** berachah being omitted, the Beis Hamikdash was destroyed and the Jewish People were exiled from their land?

The explanation appears to be that it is only if we **cherish** the Torah—only if we rejoice and delight in its sweetness—can we be sure that our children will also follow in the exalted path of the Torah and its study. It was not without reason that Chazal placed the words "*V'haarev na*—Please, make sweet" next to the supplication "May we and our descendants all know Your name and learn Your Torah for its sake," for it is only when our children witness the sweetness of Torah—its pleasure and joy—in their homes that they will also want to follow in our footsteps along the path of Torah. This is the meaning of the *pasuk* in *Haazinu*, "And this **song** shall speak up...for it shall not be forgotten from the mouths of their descendants."⁹ Only if the Torah is like a **song** in our mouths, and we passionately and fervently sing its tune, can we

---

5   *Makkos* 10a.
6   *Hilchos Rotze'ach* 7:1.
7   *Parashas Beshalach.*
8   *Berachos* 11b.
9   *Devarim* 31:21.

be assured that "…it shall not be forgotten from the mouths of their descendants."

Thus, the Baal Shem Tov stated that it was specifically the omission of *V'haarev na* that caused the land to be destroyed, the Beis Hamikdash to be razed, and the Jewish People to be exiled from their homeland.

It is in this area that we must strengthen ourselves; by increasing our joy in Torah, with song and melody, with fervor and passion, so that the Shechinah will dwell among the Jewish People.

Containing Blessing

The Second Beis Hamikdash was destroyed due to the sin of baseless hatred.[10] The *Yerushalmi*[11] relates that the people of that generation "loved money, and hated one another," as the drive to amass wealth is what leads to jealousy and baseless hatred. Only by rectifying this sin, generating feelings of peace and unity between us, will we merit the speedy rebuilding of the Beis Hamikdash.

Rashi states in *Parashas Bechukosai*:

> "*And I shall cause peace to reign in the land*"—lest we think, behold, we have food and drink…without peace, we have nothing…the pasuk teaches us, that after all else has been mentioned, "…I shall cause peace to reign in the land," from which we can see that peace is equal to everything else. Similarly, the verse states, "He Who makes peace, and creates everything."[12]

With this we can understand the statement of Chazal, "Hakadosh Baruch Hu did not find **a vessel to contain blessing** for the Jewish People except for peace."[13] Only when there is peace do food and drink, bounty and goodness have continuity and endurance, and like a vessel that protects its contents from ruin, so is peace a "vessel that contains blessing" for the Jewish People.

---

10   *Yoma* 9b.
11   Ibid. 4a.
12   *Vayikra* 26:6.
13   *Uktzin* 3:12.

Hakadosh Baruch Hu, in His great kindness, bestows upon us abundant Heavenly blessings of both spiritual and material goodness, but if we lack the "vessel to contain blessing," we will be left with nothing. This is analogous to a man for whom they poured out fine wine and fragrant oil—if his containers are cracked or his jug is leaking, none will remain. Hakadosh Baruch **Hu did not find a vessel to contain blessing for the Jewish People except for that of peace.**

Let us consider the words of the *Rambam* at the end of *Hilchos Chanukah*:[14]

> *If a person [only] has before him [the possibility of either] the [Shabbos] candles for his home or the Chanukah lights, or [alternatively] the [Shabbos] lights for his home or [wine for] Kiddush; the [Shabbos] lights take precedence, so that there may be peace in the home, for behold the Divine name is erased to make peace between a man and his wife. How great is peace, for the entire Torah was given in order to make peace in the world, as it is written, "Its ways are ways of pleasantness, and all its paths are peace."*

These words are astounding: **The entire Torah was given in order to make peace in the world!**

This is the intent of the prophet with the words, "Truth and peace shall you love." When you love truth—the Torah of truth—thus rectifying the destruction of the First Beis Hamikdash, and when you will love peace, thereby rectifying the destruction of the Second Beis Hamikdash, then, and only then, will you merit that "the fast of the fourth [month] and the fast of the fifth [month], the fast of the seventh [month] and the fast of the tenth [month], **will become for the Jewish People gladness and joy and days of festivity**," speedily in our days, *Amen*.[15]

---

14 4:14.
15 We see this point expressed further in the haftarah for *Shabbos Chazon*, in which Yeshayahu HaNavi rebukes the Jewish People for their sins and wickedness, and for the absence of justice and the lack of charity. The chapter concludes, "Tzion will be **redeemed with justice**, and its captives with **charity**." Corresponding to these two conditions, Zechariah HaNavi proclaimed, "Truth [justice] and peace [charity] shall you love."

The Words of the Netziv

While we are discussing the sin of baseless hatred, its detriment, and its grave punishment, there is great value in contemplating the introduction of the *Netziv* to his great work *Haamek Davar* on *Sefer Bereishis*. Due to their great significance, I will quote his words:

> *The praise of being "yashar" [upright] is stated to justify Hashem's destruction of the Second Beis Hamikdash, which was a crooked and perverse generation.* **We have explained that they were righteous, pious, and toiled in Torah,** *but were not upright in their general conduct, and therefore, due to the baseless hatred they felt toward one another, they suspected anyone of whom they disapproved of their fear of God to be a* **Tzeduki and apikores***. This led to copious bloodshed, together with many other tragedies, until the Beis Hamikdash was destroyed. For this reason, the judgment [of destruction] was just, for Hashem is yashar, and cannot tolerate such tzaddikim unless they are also upright in their day-to-day conduct, not if they act perversely even if their intentions are for the sake of Heaven, for this causes the destruction of Creation, and the breakdown of society.*

How penetrating are these words, and how applicable they are to us—it is as if they had been written today.

The baseless hatred that destroyed the Second Beis Hamikdash was not between unlearned people, nor between wicked, rebellious people. Rather it was between the righteous, the pious, and the scholarly. Each of these righteous individuals was sure that only his path and outlook was fit to be followed, and all other views were erroneous or even heretical.

"For Hashem is upright, and cannot tolerate such *tzaddikim!*" It is possible that they were *tzaddikim* in their Divine service, pious and scholars of Torah, but Hashem did not desire them, and because of such *tzaddikim*, the Beis Hamikdash was destroyed.

There will obviously be differences of opinion even among righteous and pious people regarding fundamental principles of *hashkafah*—there have always been disputes of this kind between Gedolei Yisrael and their followers; but this is far removed from **hatred**.

The trait of humility dictates that we understand and believe, that those who disagree with us are also righteous, and may even be greater than us in their virtue and holiness, and their viewpoint also has its place under the sun—the sun of Torah.

It is our duty to distance ourselves from these feelings of hatred and ensure that it is loathed by all those who fear the word of Hashem, and by all in whom the love and fear of Hashem dwells in their hearts.

Every *tzaddik* and *talmid chacham* is entitled to stand up for his opinion, and even to fight for it, but he has no right to hate or cause hatred. This hatred is a destructive force, which is devastating to the world of Torah and Yiddishkeit; that is what destroyed the Beis Hamikdash, burned our Sanctuary, and still dances among us.

SIX

I See an Almond Branch

> *And the word of Hashem came to me saying: "What do you see, Yirmiyahu?" And I replied, "I see an almond branch (שקד)." And Hashem told me, "You have seen well, for I am eager (שוקד) to fulfill My word."*
>
> Yirmiyahu 1:11–12

The *Yerushalmi* comments, "Just as an almond tree takes twenty-one days from when it blossoms until its fruits are fully formed, likewise, from the day that the wall was breached until the Beis Hamikdash was destroyed there were twenty-one days."[1]

It appears to me that there is another allusion in the prophecy of the almond branch. It is stated in *Maseches Maasros* that almonds are bitter.[2] Nevertheless, the Gemara asserts that an *eiruv* may be made using almonds, for they can be sweetened with "*ohr*" (literally, "light," i.e., by roasting them). The inference conveyed to Yirmiyahu was that the *churban* was to be compared to an almond branch. Almonds are bitter, but we are able to make them sweet with *ohr*—and "*ohr* only

---

1   *Taanis* 23a.
2   1:4.

refers to Torah." With the light of Torah—the Torah that is compared to fire—we can sweeten the pain of exile: "Are My words not like fire, says Hashem."[3]

We have one way to sweeten the bitterness of the *churban*—through Torah. The houses of Torah, the *batei midrash* and *batei k'nesses*, are considered miniature *Batei Mikdash*,[4] and through them we will merit the great and holy Beis Hamikdash. The Beis Hamikdash was destroyed and the land lost because they did not make a blessing before studying Torah—Torah wasn't important in their eyes and they did not study it for its own sake.[5] Only by loving the Torah and its study will we merit the rebuilding of the Beis Hamikdash.

Let us explore the words of the *Ohr Hachaim Hakadosh* at the beginning of *Parashas Tetzaveh*:

> And by way of allusion, the pasuk can be explained by the statement of the sefer Zohar Chadash (Bereishis 8), that the Jewish People are redeemed from each of the four exiles in the merit of one individual. The redemption from the first exile was in the merit of Avraham Avinu, the second in the merit of Yitzchak Avinu, the third in the merit of Yaakov Avinu, and the fourth will be in the merit of Moshe. For this reason, the exile is prolonged, for as long as they are not engaged in Torah and mitzvos, Moshe does not want to redeem a nation that is neglectful of the Torah.

It appears to me that the *Zohar*'s intent is not that Moshe is **unwilling** to redeem us, for it is inconceivable that Moshe Rabbeinu, our faithful shepherd, who bore the nation as a nursing mother bears her young, would not want to redeem Yisrael. Rather, he is **unable** to redeem them. For if we were redeemed from previous exiles in the merit of the Avos, it was clearly due to their individual merits. The exile from Egypt was due to the merit of *chessed* (kindness), the attribute of Avraham

---

3   *Yirmiyahu* 23:29.
4   *Megillah* 29a.
5   *Nedarim* 81a, see *Ran* there.

Avinu, about whom it is written, "Bestow kindness to Avraham."[6] The subsequent redemptions were in the merit of the trait of *gevurah* (inner strength) of Yitzchak, and *tiferes* (splendor) of Yaakov. If so, the redemption from the final exile will be achieved through the power of Torah, for the essence of Moshe is Torah and the Torah is ascribed to his name, as it is written, "Remember the Torah of Moshe, My servant."[7] Only when we engage in the study of Torah, and love it ceaselessly, will Moshe be given the strength to bring about the salvation of the Jewish People and the complete redemption.

"For You Hashem, set it ablaze with fire, and with fire—of Torah—will You rebuild it," speedily in our days, *Amen*.

---

[6] *Michah* 7:20.
[7] *Malachi* 3:22.

SEVEN

They Did Not Recite a Berachah before Studying Torah

Rav Yehudah stated in the name of Rav: What is the meaning of the pasuk, "Who is the wise man that can understand this"? This [question—namely, "For what reason was the land destroyed?"] was asked to the Sages, the prophets, and the angels, but they could not answer it, until Hakadosh Baruch Hu Himself explained it, as the pasuk states, "And Hashem said, 'For they forsook my Torah,' in that they did not recite a berachah before studying Torah."

Nedarim 81a

The *Ran* cites the *Megillas Setarim* of Rabbeinu Yonah, who explains that Rav Yehudah inferred that their sin was that they did not recite a berachah before Torah:

> *For if they did not study Torah at all, when the wise men and prophets were asked [the reason for the destruction of the land], why could they not explain it—surely it is clear and easily understood? Rather, they were certainly engaged constantly in the study of Torah, thus the wise men and prophets were at a loss to explain why the land was destroyed, until it was explained by Hashem Himself—who discerns the depths of man's heart—"that they did not recite a berachah before studying Torah," meaning that it was not important enough in their eyes to be worthy of a berachah; they did not study it for its own sake.*

Seemingly, the question still remains unanswered: how is it that the Sages and prophets of the Jewish People, who were keenly aware of the spiritual state of the nation, did not take note that they were no longer ascribing importance to the Torah and studying it *lishmah* (for its own sake)?[1] How did they not discern that the Jewish People were not studying Torah *lishmah*? Even if we would put these questions aside, we would have difficulty understanding why the Beis Hamikdash was destroyed on account of failing to study Torah *lishmah*. Surely Chazal state that even if Torah is studied for ulterior motives, it is still a great mitzvah; thus a person should always study Torah even *she'lo lishmah*, for by doing so, he will ultimately come to study it *lishmah*![2]

Furthermore, during the period of the *churban*, the Jews were transgressing severe sins of adultery, idolatry, and murder. In *Maseches Yoma*,[3] Chazal consider this to be the cause of the destruction, which appears to contradict the Gemara above.

To explain this passage, we will preface with the Midrashim that discuss the mitzvah of building the Beis Hamikdash—for the cause of the destruction is surely rooted in the basis of its construction. Once the

---

1   The question is even stronger with regard to the *Bach*'s version of the Gemara, which relates that even the angels couldn't explain it, despite the fact that angels are aware of a person's thoughts, as stated by *Tosafos Shabbos* 12a; see the *Noam Elimelech, Parashas Behaalosecha*.
2   *Pesachim* 50b.
3   9b.

basis of its construction and continuity are removed, its cessation and destruction follow. The *Midrash Rabbah* in *Parashas Terumah* states:

> *Is there a sale in which the seller is sold together with the item? Hashem told the Jewish People: I have sold you the Torah; I was, so to speak, sold with it, as the pasuk states, "And they shall take* **Me** *as a dedication" [literally, "And they shall take a dedication for Me"]. This is analogous to a king who had an only daughter. Another king came and married her and wished to return to his land with his wife. The king told him, "My daughter whom I gave to you is an only child, and I cannot bear to part from her. I also cannot tell you not to take her with you, because she is your wife. Rather, do me this favor; wherever you go, make me a small chamber where I can stay, for I cannot part from my daughter." Likewise, Hashem says to the Jewish People: I have given you the Torah; I cannot bear to part from it. To tell you not to take it—I [also] cannot do. But to every place you go, make Me a home where I can stay with you, as the pasuk states, "And you shall make for Me a Sanctuary."*[4]

This Midrash greatly illuminates the concept of the Shechinah residing among the Jewish People. "I cannot bear to part from it," says Hashem. Wherever Hashem's Torah is found and studied, His Shechinah can be found. The bestowing of the Torah upon the Jewish People was the reason Hashem commanded, "Make for Me a Sanctuary and I shall dwell among you." With this in mind, we can gain a new insight into the words of Rabbi Chalafta ben Dosa, "How do we know that even one person [who studies Torah, the Shechinah resides with him]? The *pasuk* states, 'Every place in which you will mention My name, I will come to you and bless you.'"[5] For any place in which the Torah is studied

---

4   33:1. See the *Ramban*'s commentary to the beginning of *Parashas Terumah*, where he explains that the presence of the Shechinah in the Sanctuary was a continuation of the glory of Hashem that resided on Har Sinai at *Matan Torah*. In light of this Midrash, his words are beautifully elucidated.

5   *Avos* 3:6.

properly, even by an individual, Hashem, so to speak, says, "I cannot bear to part from it."

The *Zohar* states:

> How precious is the Torah before Hashem, for in every place in which words of Torah are heard, Hashem and all His assembly listen to its words, and Hashem comes and dwells upon the person, as it is written, "In every place in which you mention My name…"[6]

However, there seems to be an issue with the aforementioned parable, for the analogy does not match the message that it seeks to communicate. When a person marries off his daughter, she will understandably leave her father's home to live with her husband, for a person cannot be in two places at once. Similarly, an ordinary gift must transfer from the giver to the recipient, for if it belongs to one, it does not belong to the other. The words of the king, "My daughter is an only child, and I cannot part from her" are surely correct; however, a person who teaches wisdom and knowledge to another does not lose it thereby—a teacher does not need to depart from his wisdom to give it to another. He and his student can understand and comprehend it together. If so, why did Hashem tell the Jewish People, "I cannot bear to part from it," and why did He thus instruct the building of a Sanctuary in the lower realms?

In truth, when Hashem gave the Torah to the Jewish People, it wasn't just "wisdom and intellect" to study and teach, to understand and comprehend. Rather, He gave them the Torah as a possession over which to exercise dominion, and with which to exercise dominion over all Creation. Since the Torah was given to us, we do not pay attention to a *Bas Kol* (a Heavenly voice), for "The Torah is not in the Heavens, for it was already given at Har Sinai." When there was a dispute between Rabbi Eliezer and Rabbi Yehoshua regarding the *tanur shel achnai*,[7] Rabbi Eliezer's view was not accepted even though the foundations of nature were shaken—a carob tree was uprooted from its place, a stream flowed

---

6   3, 118a.
7   *Bava Metzia* 59b.

backward, and the walls of the *beis midrash* started to cave in. Even when a *Bas Kol* emanated from the Heavens to verify the correct view, saying, "What do you have against Rabbi Eliezer, for the halachah always follows his opinion," his view was still not accepted. And when Rabbi Yehoshua arose and declared, "The Torah is not in the Heavens," the halachah was affirmed then and for all time, that Hashem gave the Torah to the Jewish People, and gave their Sages the authority to decide its halachos, and to instruct the nation as to the path they should follow, and the manner in which they should act.

A further dimension to this is evident in *Bava Metzia*:

> There was a dispute in the Heavenly Yeshiva [regarding the halachos of tzaraas]: If the baheres precedes the white hair, [the person] is tamei (impure); if the white hair precedes the baheres, he is tahor (pure). If it is a case of doubt, Hashem says he is tahor, and the entire Heavenly Academy say he is tamei. They said: Who can decide? Let Rabbah bar Nachmeni decide, for Rabbah bar Nachmeni declared, "I am unique in Nega'im, I am unique in Ohalos." They sent a messenger to him, but the Angel of Death couldn't approach him because he did not cease from his study. In the meantime, a wind blew and rattled between the branches. He thought it was a band of Persians and said, "Let that man rather die and not fall into the hands of the authorities." When his spirit was departing, he pronounced, "It is pure, it is pure." A Bas Kol emanated and declared,[8] "Praiseworthy are you, Rabbah bar Nachmeni, for your body is pure, and your soul departed with [the word] 'pure.'"[9]

We see that there was a dispute between Hashem and the Heavenly Yeshiva as to whether the halachah in a certain case of *tum'as nega'im* is *tamei* or *tahor*, and Rabbah bar Nachmeni, who was authorized to settle this dispute, ruled that it is *tahor*, as Hashem opined. Nevertheless, the

---

8   See *D'rashos HaRan*, *d'rush* 5, in regard to this statement of Chazal.
9   86a.

Rambam rules in *Hilchos Tzaraas*, that the halachah in this case is *tamei*.[10] The *Kesef Mishneh* explains astoundingly, "Since he stated this at the time that his soul was departing, it is included in the rule that [the Torah] is not in the Heavens, and it is not sufficient to override the rule that the halachah follows the *Tanna Kama*." Truly astonishing words!

Consider the extent of the *koach haTorah* (power of Torah) that Hashem, in His abundant mercy, gave over to the Jewish People a power that can, so to speak, overrule the Divine view.

Not only did Hashem give the Jewish People authority regarding the Torah, He even gave them the capacity to rule over nature, as stated in the *Yerushalmi*: "A three-year-old girl who had intercourse, her signs of virginity do not return; if the *beis din* rule and declare a leap year, her signs of virginity return, this [concept is expressed by the *pasuk*], 'Hashem fulfills for me.'"[11]

Hashem handed over His world to those who toil in and study Torah in purity; to control and even change its course through their halachic rulings.

It is in regard to the amazing capacity granted to the Jewish People to add and develop novel ideas in Torah with their intellect, and to exercise authority over its halachos that Hashem says, "I have given you My Torah, I cannot part from it; rather in every place that you go, make Me a chamber that I may dwell with you." Hashem removed, so to speak, this power from Himself, and gave it to the Jewish People.

With this, we can understand the statement of Chazal, "Hashem only made a covenant with the Jewish People due to the Oral Law, as it says, 'For by the word of these oral matters [literally, on account of these matters], I have made a covenant with you and with the Jewish People.'"[12] This calls for comment: What is the special quality of the Oral Law over the Written Law such that the covenant cast between Hashem and the Jewish People was only due to the Oral Law? In light of the above, the answer is startlingly simple; for the covenant with the

---

10   2:9.
11   *Nedarim* 6:8, cited by the *Shach*, *Yoreh Deah* 189:13.
12   *Gittin* 60b.

Jewish People, and the Divine presence residing in their midst, pertains to the Oral Law, which contains the *koach* of the Jewish People to exercise authority over Torah, to analyze and add their portion, regarding which Hashem says, "I cannot part from it."

Pilpul, Moshe Rabbeinu, and the Jewish People

With this in mind, we can understand the statement of Chazal that the power of *pilpul* (analytical exposition of Torah) was given to Moshe and his descendants alone, but he benevolently handed it over to the whole of the Jewish People.[13] Now, surely Hashem wanted this capacity to be given to the Jewish People, for it is one of the foundational acquisitions of Torah, as stated in the *Beraisa* of *Kinyan Torah*.[14] If so, why was it originally given only to Moshe? In light of the above, we may suggest that Hashem desired that the capacity of *pilpul* should belong to the Jewish People. He therefore gave this *koach* to Moshe so that he should give it as a complete acquisition to them, thereby causing the Shechinah to dwell among them—when the Divine will would arise, saying, "The Torah that I have given you, I cannot part from it."

The *Haamek Davar* at the beginning of *Parashas Tetzaveh* states that the *shefa* (Divine influence) of Torah to the Jewish nation flows through two of the vessels of the *Mishkan*—the *Aron* and the *Menorah*. However, there is an intrinsic difference between the two. The *Aron*, containing the *Luchos*, represents the Torah that was handed over at Har Sinai. The *Menorah* is the fount of the power of *chiddush* (expounding novel thoughts) and *pilpul* in the Torah. (Rabbi Tarfon used to refer to a good *chiddush* as "*kaftor va'ferach*," referring to the knobs and flowers that decorated the *Menorah*, in allusion to this concept that the power of *chiddush* in Torah is bestowed via the knobs and flowers of the golden *Menorah*.)[15]

With this in mind, we can understand why the *Menorah* was the only vessel crafted by Moshe, whereas the other vessels—even the

---

13   *Nedarim* 38a.
14   *Avos* 6.
15   See *Bereishis Rabbah* 91:10.

Aron—were made by Betzalel, as the *pasuk* states, "And Betzalel made the *Aron* out of cedar wood."[16] The *Menorah*, however, was manufactured by Moshe, as the *Midrash Tanchuma* relates: Moshe had difficulty in the manufacture of the *Menorah*, until Hashem told him to take a talent of gold and throw it into the furnace, and immediately, the completed *Menorah* emerged.[17] Although the *Menorah* was Divinely formed, it came about through Moshe's act of throwing the talent of gold into the fire. It appears that this was because the power of *pilpul* and *chiddush* emanated through the *Menorah*, and this was given to Moshe who, in his generosity, gave it over to the Jewish People.

In this light, perhaps we may understand the puzzling statement of the Gemara, that when Moshe Rabbeinu saw Rabbi Akiva expounding numerous halachos from the crown of every letter, he said, "Master of the World, You have a person like this, yet You give the Torah through me?"[18] This needs explanation—why was Rabbi Akiva's brilliance in *pilpul* and *chiddush* relevant to the question of the Torah being given through Moshe? In light of the above, we may explain that Moshe made the following argument to Hashem: "Rabbi Akiva, whose power in the 'battle of Torah' is so great that he expounds on every crown (see *Rashi*, "Once Rabbi Akiva died, the warriors of Torah ceased"[19]—the depth of reasoning, [the ability] to connect the logic of the Oral Torah to the expositions of the *pesukim*), is surely more suitable than me to receive the *pilpul* of Torah and give it over to the Jewish People."

According to the *Nefesh Hachaim*,[20] as well as the *Chasam Sofer*,[21] Torah *lishmah* is the study of the *pilpul* and logic of Torah with great joy and pleasure. Even according to the disciples of the Baal Shem Tov, who explain the parameters of *lishmah* differently, the preferred and most significant study of Torah is that which is studied with joy and pleasure, out of the sweetness and pleasantness of its *pilpul*. In the

---

16   *Shemos* 37:1.
17   *Behaalosecha* 4.
18   *Menachos* 29b.
19   *Sotah* 49b.
20   4:3.
21   *Nedarim* 81a and commentary to *Parashas Bechukosai*.

introduction to his *sefer Eglei Tal*, the holy Gaon of Sochatchov cites the *Zohar* that the *yetzer hatov* grows from the joy of Torah. Since this form of Torah study develops the *yetzer hatov*, it is surely the main path of Torah learning. The *sefer Degel Machaneh Ephraim* cites his grandfather the Baal Shem Tov,[22] who said that when Chazal state that the second *churban* occurred because "they did not recite a blessing before studying Torah," they referred to the blessing "*V'haarev na*," which relates to the sweetness and pleasantness of Torah—like honey to the mouth.

By way of allusion, it may be suggested that this is one of the reasons that Torah is compared to water, as stated by Chazal.[23] Water is given most significance when it is drunk by a person who is thirsty, otherwise a berachah is not recited upon drinking it.[24] This also applies to Torah; the primary manner of Torah study is that accompanied by great pleasure and joy.

Apart from the inherent greatness and importance of toil and *chiddush* in Torah, doing so also gives great honor to the Torah, for it implants in the hearts of those who study it that "no part of it is in vain."[25] Furthermore, it shows that great toil is required to understand each concept properly, whether the written *pesukim* of Torah, or the reasoning of Chazal, expounded by means of their Divine inspiration and profound wisdom, broader than the land and deeper than the sea—if only we would be worthy of understanding a fraction of their breadth of knowledge and logic.

The Power of Torah Lishmah

Since the Shechinah resides in Yisrael due to the study of Torah *lishmah*, it follows that when Yisrael are not studying Torah as they should, the Shechinah no longer resides among them. This is not a punishment; rather when the causative force ceases, the effect stops automatically. The basis for the Shechinah residing among the Jewish People is Torah; when the sound of Torah ceases from Yisrael, the Shechinah no longer

---

22 *Parashas Beshalach.*
23 *Bava Kama* 17a.
24 *Tosafos, Berachos* 45a.
25 As explained by *Rashi* in *Sotah* loc. cit.

resides among them. A further dimension is evident from the *Tzelach* at the end of *Maseches Berachos*, who states that before a person recites the berachos over Torah, the Torah belongs to Hashem. Only once he recites the berachah is Torah given to him as a gift and becomes his Torah. In this light, we may say that it is specifically the blessings over the Torah, which bring it into the domain of the Jewish People, that cause Hashem to say, "I cannot bear to part from it," and therefore causes His Shechinah to reside in Yisrael.

This is analogous to a king who loved the music played by one of his servants who was a professional violinist. Morning, afternoon, and evening, the king would enjoy the beautiful tones of his violin. One day, the violinist committed a grave sin against the king and was sentenced to death. The king requested of the judges that the verdict be reconsidered, for although they surely judged correctly and the violinist deserved the death penalty, the king's life was not a life without the sweet tones of the violin, and he—the king—did not deserve to be punished. When the judges heard the heartfelt words of the king, they were moved, and immediately agreed to postpone their verdict so that the king could continue to enjoy the pleasant sounds of his beloved violin. Sometime later, the violinist contracted an illness that disabled his hand and made him unable to play any longer, and the sounds of his music ceased from the king's courtyard. The judges reconvened and decided that since his music no longer gave pleasure to the king, there was no longer any reason to postpone his verdict, and he was sent to his death.[26]

Similarly, during the times of the *churban*, the decree of exile and destruction was made due to the cardinal sins of idolatry, adultery, and murder, as stated by the Gemara.[27] However, as long as the sound of Torah *lishmah* ascended from the synagogues and houses of study in Yisrael, "Love covers over all transgressions,"[28] and the King of Kings declared, "I cannot bear to be separated from it." However, when the

---

26 See responsa *Maharit*, sec. 1, 100.
27 *Yoma* 9b.
28 *Mishlei* 10:12.

stage was reached whereby "Torah was not important in their eyes, and they did not study it *lishmah*," there was no longer any reason to delay the terrible and frightening decree, and then the glory was exiled from our Beis Hamikdash, the Beis Hamikdash was destroyed, and the Shechinah departed from Yisrael.

This matter was asked to the Sages, prophets, and angels, yet they could not explain it, for they did not have the wherewithal to explain it. They certainly knew that the Jewish People were no longer studying Torah *lishmah*, but they did not see this to be a reason for the *churban*, for "a person should always study Torah and perform mitzvos even for ulterior motives." Finally, Hashem himself explained it, revealing that the basis for the residing of the Shechinah is "I cannot bear to part from it [Torah]." Once the sweet and beloved sound of Torah—which covered over all their sins—was no longer present, the decree was enacted, "For having forsaken the Torah that I placed before them."[29]

In this light, we can understand the esoteric statement of the *Yerushalmi*: "Rabbi Yannai said: Had the Torah been given as clear-cut rulings, the world would not be able to endure."[30] This statement is not elaborated upon in the commentaries there. The explanation appears to be that had the Torah been given in a simple and straightforward format, without need for the *pilpul* of Torah; the assertion that "I cannot bear to part from it" would not apply, and there would be no reason for the presence of the Shechinah in the Beis Hamikdash.

Toiling in Torah with Joy

Based on the above, the words of the *Zohar* shine with a new light. "From the day the Beis Hamikdash was destroyed and the sacrifices ceased, all that Hashem has in the world are these words of Torah and the Torah that is **expounded in his [the *talmid chacham*'s] mouth**."[31]

For regarding the Torah of Yisrael—the aspect of Torah that was given to them as a full acquisition—to rule over, to expound, and explain its

---

29 See *Taz, Orach Chaim* 47:1, who expresses a similar idea.
30 *Sanhedrin* 21a.
31 *Zohar, Parashas Balak*.

concepts with *pilpul* and logic—Hashem says, "I cannot be separated from it," and because of this aspect of Torah, Hashem cast a covenant with the Jewish People and resided His Shechinah among them.

The *Zohar* teaches us the great value of the *chiddushei Torah* that are propounded in every generation by rabbis and their students, about which it is stated that they are all Hashem has in His world. The main joy and delight of Torah learning is found when a student toils to understand the depth of Torah and its eternal beauty. We are commanded to delight in Torah in the same way that Hashem delights in it, as Rabbeinu Yonah states:

> "And when you toil in Torah, delight in it," for we find that the Torah declares, "Hashem created me, the first of His path, before His works of then," and it is written, "And I was a nursling to Him and I was His delight every day." We thus see that Hashem delights in it, and so should we, as it states, "A source of joy in His inhabited land, and delight among people"—meaning that just as the Torah was the delight of Hashem before the creation of the world, so shall it be a source of joy after the world was created, and a delight for people.[32]

Rabbeinu Yonah's words are sweeter than honey and are a great lesson to those who study and toil over Torah in purity. Generally, people view "toil" and "delight" as contradictory: it is only when a person rests from his toil that he engages in enjoyable pursuits. However, this is not the case regarding the nation of Hashem and His Torah, for our toil is unlike the toil of the other nations and our delight is unlike theirs. The Torah is the object of our toil—but also our delight and joy. There is no greater pleasure in Torah than *pilpul* and *chiddush* in its principles, and the toil to understand the depth of its ways. This is the power of "the Torah that is expounded in his mouth."

It is stated that "there is no joy like clarifying doubts" and, moreover, it is a person's nature to be impressed and inspired by a *chiddush* that

---

32 *Avos* 2:14.

illuminates an area in which he had previously been in the dark. It appears that this is the meaning of the statement of David HaMelech, "I rejoice over your words like one who finds a great treasure."[33] The main joy is in the **discovery** of the treasure, not in its usage, which is only a source of benefit—not of rejoicing. David delighted and rejoiced in the treasure and bounty that he found in the Torah every day, as *Rashi* comments, "On one of your statements that was unclear—once I understood it."[34]

I heard from my teacher, the Klausenberger Rebbe, *zt"l*, an explanation of the *pasuk*, "They are more desirable than gold and a fortune of purest gold, and sweeter than honey and honeycomb."[35] The body receives no pleasure from the actual attainment of wealth, but silver and gold are things that enable the attainment of any pleasure or desire. Conversely, the body gets pleasure from the consumption of honey and sweet-tasting food, but they have no enduring benefit. Torah study contains both qualities. The Torah is more desirable than gold, and there is no measure to the greatness of their wondrous and astounding qualities, and the greatness of the reward of those who study it. The Torah protects and saves. At the same time, it is sweeter than honey, and there is no end to the pleasure of studying it. All the Sages of Yisrael throughout the generations cleaved to Torah study and found limitless pleasure therein. In the introduction written by the sons of the *Vilna Gaon* to his commentary on the *Shulchan Aruch, Orach Chaim*, amazing and astounding accounts of the greatness of the *Gaon*'s commitment to

---

33 *Tehillim* 119:162.
34 It is clear that David delved deeply into the practical areas of the Torah like all of our forefathers, who did not cease from Torah study. We also see this from his request that the study of *Tehillim* be considered like the study of *Nega'im* and *Ohalos*. See the *Rambam*'s introduction to *Zera'im*, where he states, "That which Yehoshua and Pinchas did with analysis and logic was the same as what was done by Ravina and Rav Ashi." Chazal in *Megillah* 16a state that Mordechai studied the laws of *Kemitzah*, and in *Chullin* 44b they cite a law in *hilchos treifos* from Yonah HaNavi (see the gloss of the *Beis Yosef* and the comment of *Rashi*). In *Chullin* 137b, they state that Rabbi Yosi said over a teaching in the name of Chagai, Zechariah, and Malachi regarding *reishis ha'geiz*, likewise in *Bechoros* 58a and *Yevamos* 16a, regarding the words of Chagai (see *Nazir* 53a).
35 *Tehillim* 19:11.

Torah, exceeding human nature, are described. All of these Gedolim fulfilled the words of the *Rambam*, "The lives of the masters and seekers of wisdom are considered like death without Torah study."[36]

---

36   *Hilchos Rotze'ach* 7:1.

EIGHT

They Loved Money and Hated One Another

> *We have found that the First Beis Hamikdash was destroyed because they were idol worshippers, adulterers, and murderers. However [at the time of] the second [destruction], we know that they toiled in Torah, were careful in mitzvah observance and the separation of tithes, and possessed every good trait. But they loved money and had baseless hatred for one another. Baseless hatred is a grave matter, for it is equated to idolatry, adultery, and murder.*
>
> Yerushalmi, Yoma 1:1, 4b

"They loved money—but hated one another." These two ideas are dependent on one another. Pursuing financial gain is interlinked with brotherly hatred. We know from life experience that there is nothing more potent than the love of money in causing rifts between friends and in shattering families. Brothers who have lived together in harmony for years receive their father's inheritance, and the money becomes a source of dispute between them, until ultimately, they cut all ties with each other, and become bitter enemies.

This is why Chazal spoke so very critically of those who pursue money. In fact, they went so far as to say that the desire for wealth is not only a stumbling block regarding interpersonal mitzvos, but even prevents a person from ascending in levels of *kedushah*. He will only grow in matters of *kedushah* when he learns to despise money and nullify it in his heart like the dust of the earth.

Let us take note of the following statement of the *Yerushalmi*: "Why was [Rabbi Yehudah HaNasi] called Rabbeinu **HaKadosh**? Because he never looked at his *milah* in his life. And why was [Nachum] called Nachum Ish **Kodesh Kodashim**? Because **he never looked at a coin in his life.**"[1]

Rabbeinu HaKadosh attained ten levels of holiness because he never looked at his *milah*, and became sanctified with the *middah* of *yesod*, purity of eyes and thought. However, Nachum Ish Kodesh Kodashim surpassed him twofold in levels of *kedushah*, because he never looked at a coin—all the money in the world was worthless in his eyes.

Hold on to this *mussar* and do not let it go!

Raising Children on Honest Money

The punishment for benefiting from money unjustly is exceptionally severe. Aside from the statement of Chazal that those who lend money with interest lose their assets, great *tzaddikim* have taught us that a person's sons and daughters are spiritually affected when they are raised and supported by money attained dishonestly. My teacher, the Klausenberger Rebbe, *zt"l*, would frequently mention (and wrote in his *tzavaah*), the words of the *Agra D'Pirka*:

> His honor, our master, the holy Rav Menachem Mendel would note that it is puzzling that we frequently see children who, in their youth, go to their rebbeim's homes and learn with diligence,

---

1 Sanhedrin 53b; Avodah Zarah 18a.

daven with intent, answer "Amen Yehei Shemei Rabba" and "Amen," and conduct themselves properly. However, when they grow older, they develop bad character traits and neglect Torah study, tefillah, and similar matters. How could such a thing occur? Surely, the Torah they learned in their youth was "breath without sin" (Shabbos 119b), and should have stood in their stead, increasing their spiritual vigor, for one mitzvah leads to another. He answered that it is due to their fathers providing for them with stolen money, earned through dishonest business dealings. The forbidden matters they ate became part of their flesh, which led to their developing negative traits and desires. He brought proof to this from the crop of a bird, that on account of deriving benefit from stolen food, is not offered on the Mizbei'ach for it is not favorable. Although the bird was never commanded in the prohibition, Hashem hates stealing.[2]

If we would only be wise enough to understand this. Our orphaned generation suffers from the affliction of "dropouts," as many children who grew up in fine homes suddenly distance themselves from their parents and go astray. We ask ourselves, "Why? What caused this to happen?" But, behold, a holy man has spoken; the *tzaddik* Rav Menachem Mendel of Rimanov, and he reveals the reason: He who raises his children with stolen and ill-gotten money plants within them the seeds of damage, may Hashem have mercy.

---

2   Sec. 126.

NINE

Emunah and Bitachon in Times of Divine Concealment

We are entering the month of Av, a time in which we reduce our level of joy and mourn for the destruction of the Beis Hamikdash and for the exile of the Jewish People. Even today, danger hovers over our heads and Jewish blood is spilled like water. We must strengthen our *emunah* and *bitachon* and be aware that the continuity of the Jewish People is not natural but supernatural. Hashem has assured us that "[the Torah] will not be forgotten from their descendants,"[1] and for every misfortune that occurs, we must train ourselves to say, "All that Hashem does is for the good."[2]

This is how the holy Jewish People have conducted themselves in every generation, throughout the lengthy exile. Even during difficult times of Divine concealment, when darkness covered the land, they strengthened themselves in their faith, cast their burden upon Hashem, and yearned for His salvation. In this vein, I have always explained a passage of Gemara in *Avodah Zarah*:

---

1   *Devarim* 31:21.
2   *Berachos* 60b.

> [The Romans] caught Rabbi Chanina ben Teradyon sitting and studying Torah, gathering groups in public with a Sefer Torah resting in his lap. They brought him and wrapped his Sefer Torah around him, surrounded him with bundles of twigs, and set them on fire. They took tufts of wool, soaked them in water, and placed them on his chest so that he should not die quickly. His students asked him, "Rebbi, what do you see?" He replied, "The parchment is burned, but the letters are flying into the air."[3]

Tosafos find difficulty with Rabbi Chanina's students' question, "What do you see?" Why should they suppose that he saw something? Were I not afraid to suggest it, I would say that their question did not pertain to something visible to the eyes, but to something perceived by the intellect and heart. Those were days of wrath, a bleak period of harsh decrees and destruction, with the calamities of each passing day surpassing those that preceded it, until the leader of the generation, in whose protective shadow the people had thought to survive, ascended Heavenward in a storm. In their cry of despair, the desperate question burst forth from their broken hearts, "Rebbi, what do you see?" Is there hope for us left as a flock without a shepherd?

Rabbi Chanina ben Teradyon replied that their spirits should not fall, and that they should not be downhearted, for there is hope to our future, and purpose to our perseverance. "The parchment is being burned"—the evil kingdom can burn and destroy our bodies, but the spirit of the Jewish nation is indestructible. "The letters are flying in the air," for every Jew is likened to a *Sefer Torah*, as the Gemara states, "Someone who is present at a person's demise must tear *keriah*. To what is this comparable? To a person who sees a *Sefer Torah* being burned."[4] The body is compared to the parchment of a *Sefer Torah*, as explained by the *Beis Halevi*,[5] who states that the body of a *talmid chacham* is

---

3   18a.
4   *Shabbos* 105b.
5   Responsa, vol. 1, Introduction.

like the parchment of a *Sefer Torah*, and the souls of the Jewish nation are connected to the letters, as evident in the writings of the *Me'or Einayim*,[6] *Kedushas Levi*,[7] and *Nefesh Hachaim*.[8] This idea is also discussed by the *P'nei Yehoshua*,[9] who cites the *Zohar* that the word "ישראל" stands for "יש ששים רבוא אותיות לתורה"—There are six-hundred thousand letters in the Torah," as every Jew is connected to one of the letters of the Torah. (Thus, a person who is present at a Jew's demise, when the body expires and the soul flies away, is considered to have seen a *Sefer Torah* burn and its letters fly away.) And when Hashem wills it, the letters will be returned and reaffixed, and multitudes will once again be gathered in public to learn Torah, for Hashem has promised that it will not be forgotten from their descendants. And it was specifically this conduct of self-sacrifice, beyond nature and reason, that brought about the downfall of the Roman Empire and the salvation of the Jewish People, as evident in *Avodah Zarah*: "At the event of Rabbi Chanina ben Teradyon's execution, a decree of great destruction was issued against the Roman empire."[10] This is truly an astounding idea!

In the merit of the Jewish People's self-sacrifice for Torah, even during times of darkness and Divine concealment, Hashem will reveal the Divine presence of His might, redeem them, and bring about their salvation for all to see.

With this idea we can explain the following Gemara in *Yoma*: "Miracles occurred with the doors of Nikanor, and they would mention him favorably."[11]

The Gemara also states: "Therefore, all the gates in the Beis Hamikdash were replaced with those of gold, except for the Gates of Nikanor, for miracles were performed for them."[12]

---

6 *Parashas Va'eschanan*.
7 *Parashas Bamidbar*.
8 4:11.
9 Kiddushin 30.
10 2b, *Tosafos*, in the name of the *Maaseh Merkavah*.
11 Yoma 37a.
12 Ibid. 38a.

This is difficult to understand. Miracles were hardly out of the ordinary in the Beis Hamikdash; ten wondrous miracles occurred on a regular basis.[13] The Gemara in *Menachos* also states that sunlight didn't shine into the Beis Hamikdash at all; on the contrary, a great light shone forth outward in a miraculous fashion.[14] The Gemara in *Megillah* relates that the *Aron* did not take up any space,[15] which was an astonishing miracle, and many others are mentioned in *Yoma*.[16] If so, why did they refrain from replacing the Gates of Nikanor due to the miracles that were performed for them?

The answer seems to lie in the story related by the Gemara regarding the doors of Nikanor:

> *When Nikanor went to bring his doors from Alexandria in Egypt, on his return journey, a storm arrived that threatened to sink the ship. They took one of the doors and cast it into the sea, but the storm didn't abate. They wanted to cast the second door overboard as well. Upon seeing this, Nikanor wrapped himself around the door and said, "Cast me into the water with it!" All the while, he was distressed over the loss of the first door. When they arrived at the port of Akko, [the missing door] emerged from beneath the ship.*

On the surface, this action of Nikanor is one of panic and desperation. Surely, he realized that he would be unable to persuade the other passengers to risk their lives in order to save his doors. Further, Nikanor did not even request that the door not be thrown overboard, but held on to it and declared, "Cast me into the sea together with it!" What would he gain by acting in this way? He would also be cast into the sea and drown together with the door! However, in reality, Nikanor taught us a great lesson. When a storm arises that threatens to drown us, it necessitates *mesirus nefesh* beyond all logic and reason. This was a lesson

---

13 *Avos* 5:5
14 86b.
15 10b.
16 21a.

for all generations; namely, that during times of wrath and anger, dark and treacherous times, when it seems that mighty storms are again arising to destroy us and to drown the remnant of the Jewish People, and "experts" from our midst stand up and advocate that the doors of the Sanctuary must be cast into the sea, we must wrap ourselves around these doors and declare, "Cast us into the sea together with them," as Nikanor did in his day. To preserve this message, Nikanor's doors were not replaced with gold ones.

This obligation has been placed upon us during these times of Divine concealment at the End of Days. After one door has already been removed from us—the "Gate of *Avodah*"—and cast into the sea with the destruction of the Beis Hamikdash, we must hold fast to the remaining door—the "Gate of *Torah*"—with *mesirus nefesh* beyond all reason, with fierce love and unending joy, until we merit to witness the remaining gate emerging from beneath the ship, at the time of the fulfillment of the prophecy, "And the glory of Hashem will be revealed, and all flesh will see together that the mouth of Hashem has spoken,"[17] speedily in our days, *Amen*.

---

17   *Yeshayahu* 40:5.

TEN

She Weeps Incessantly at Night

> *She weeps incessantly at night, and her tear is on her cheek, she has no one to comfort her from all her lovers, all her friends have betrayed her, have become her enemies.*
>
> *Eichah 1:2*

> *"At night"—why at night? Because sound only travels far at night, therefore it is written, "At night." Rabbi Eivo said: [Lament at] night draws along the lament [of those who hear it]. It happened that a woman who lived in the neighborhood of Rabban Gamliel had a young son who died, and she would weep for him at night. Rabban Gamliel would hear her weeping and would remember the destruction of the Beis Hamikdash, and would weep together with her, until his eyelashes fell out.*
>
> *Eichah Rabbah 1:24*

This seems puzzling: What connection is there between the bereaved woman's pain and the destruction of the Beis Hamikdash? Surely, it was the pain of an individual, a personal tragedy, and indeed, whose heart would not break upon hearing the cries of a Jewish mother over the death of her young son?

But what does that have to do with the destruction of the Beis Hamikdash?

There was somebody who suggested that in fact, there is no direct connection between the cries of this woman and the destruction of the Beis Hamikdash, but Rabban Gamliel used her bitter cries to stimulate himself to recall the *churban* and mourn over it.

However, there are two problems with this approach. First, if Chazal attached this story to the *pasuk*, "She weeps incessantly at night, and her tear is on her cheek," we may assume that there is an intrinsic connection between this woman's pain and the pain of the *churban*, for the explanations and allusions of the *pesukim* are not about unrelated incidents. Furthermore, Chazal stated that Rabban Gamliel would hear the cries of this woman and **weep together with her**. This indicates that he shared in her pain and wept with her.

The explanation of this matter seems to be as follows. The Beis Hamikdash is not just for offering sacrifices, but to be the residing place of the Shechinah—the "House of His footstool." The Shechinah residing among us means that Hashem radiates His countenance toward His beloved children, an expression of the Attribute of Mercy. When the Attribute of Mercy presides over the Jewish People, they merit a good and long life, and experience only goodness and kindness.

Conversely, not only did the destruction of the Beis Hamikdash terminate the offerings of the daily sacrifices, it also caused the retraction of the Divine presence. The absence of the Shechinah brings Divine concealment, which is an expression of the Attribute of Justice, and when the Attribute of Justice rules, our lives are full of suffering and pain.

That is the significance of the prophecy of Zechariah HaNavi: "So says Hashem, Lord of Hosts: Elderly men and women will once again sit in the streets of Yerushalayim, each with their staff in their hand due to old age, and the streets of the city will be filled with boys and girls playing in its streets."[1]

For when the redemption comes, and the Shechinah will dwell among the Jewish People once again, we will experience lives of longevity and good health; elderly men and women with sticks in hand, and boys and girls playing in the streets.

This is the explanation of Rabban Gamliel's cries. When he heard his neighbor crying at night over her deceased young son, he saw in these cries an expression of the *churban*. For if they would have merited the Divine presence, this boy would have been playing in the streets of Yerushalayim with the other Jewish children and would not have died. The fact that they had not merited it and this bereaved woman was weeping for her young son could only be because Hashem had hidden His face and removed His presence from the Jewish People.

Thus, Chazal reference the *pasuk*, "She weeps incessantly at night, and her tear is on her cheek."

These words have added significance to us, for our generation finds it very challenging to mourn for Yerushalayim and the Beis Hamikdash. During the *Yamim Nora'im*, we see the faithful among us filled with worry and dread, overcome with the fear of judgment. However, this is not the case when it comes to the Three Weeks or even Tishah B'Av. Everyone conducts himself correctly and follows the halachos of the day, but few are those who actually feel a tangible level of pain and mourning. Certain righteous and pious individuals—a precious few—actually feel the pain of the Shechinah in exile and connect to that pain, but not everyone can reach such lofty levels, and the general populace do not relate to it.

However, in light of the above, each individual can clearly feel the pain of the *churban* and can easily mourn for the Beis Hamikdash. For many are the "neighbors of Rabban Gamliel," and to our sorrow, there is barely a home that is unscathed. In every city and community, a woman weeps over her young son, a young man struggles with a serious illness,

---

1   *Zechariah* 8:4–5.

and many other calamities befall us. Anyone who bends his ear can hear Rabban Gamliel's neighbor weeping at night and weep together with her over the pain of the Jewish People, the Divine concealment, and the Attribute of Justice that presides over the Jewish People.

ELEVEN

You Are Children to Hashem Your God

The Rabbis taught: When the Second Beis Hamikdash was destroyed, many Jews refrained from eating meat or drinking wine. Rabbi Yehoshua engaged with them, and asked, "My sons, why are you not eating meat or drinking wine?" They replied, "Should we eat meat, which used to be sacrificed on the Altar, and is now discontinued? Should we drink wine, which used to be poured as libations on the Altar, and is now discontinued?" He told them, "If so, we should not eat bread, because the Menachos (meal-offerings) have been discontinued." [They replied,] "It is possible to eat fruit." [He said to them,] "We should not eat fruit, for the Bikkurim have been discontinued." [They replied,] "It is possible to eat other fruit." [He said to them,] "We should not drink water, for the water libations have been discontinued." They remained silent. He told them, "My sons,

> to tell you not to mourn at all is not possible, for the [Divine] decree has been enacted, but to mourn too much is not possible, for a decree is only made if the majority of the congregation are capable of upholding it."
>
> *Bava Basra 60a*

> *You are children to Hashem your God, do not gash yourselves, and do not make a bald patch between your eyes on account of a death.*
>
> *Devarim 14:1*

We find two explanations of this *pasuk* in the Rishonim:

"Children"—once you know that you are children to Hashem, and He loves you more than a father loves a son, do not gash yourselves on account of anything that might happen, for all that He does is for the good. And if you do not understand it, in the same way that young children do not understand what their father does, but rely on him regardless, so should you act, for you are a holy nation, and are not like the Canaanites, and you should therefore not act as they do.[1]

"You are children to Hashem your God, do not gash yourselves"—for it is inappropriate to display an extreme level of sorrow and pain over a deceased relative, when he leaves behind another relative more honorable in stature and who may be relied upon to do good. Thus, you—who are children to Hashem, your Father, Who exists forever—it is inappropriate that you should express such extreme sorrow and mourning over any death.[2]

---

1   Ibn Ezra.
2   Seforno.

We are commanded to mourn over a death. This was practiced by our forefather Avraham before the Torah was given: "And Sarah died in Kiryas Arba, which is Chevron, in the Land of Canaan, and Avraham arrived to eulogize Sarah and to cry for her."[3] The *Ramban* comments, "The Torah does not forbid weeping [over a death], **for a person's nature is aroused to weep at the separation from his loved ones even when they are alive.**"[4]

Let us consider the exceedingly wise words of the *Radvaz*, with regard to someone who did not cry throughout the mourning period for his departed son:

> *Question: Regarding one of the great men of the generation who lost a son and did not shed a tear over him—is this a good trait or not? Answer: This is a bad trait, which reflects a hardened heart and a bad nature. It is a trait of cruelty, and the view of the philosophers who maintain that all of this world is a work of deception—may they be reduced beyond nothingness, and their memory be like those likened to despicable dust. Therefore, do not be persuaded by their sin and their axioms, for they are all based on this premise. However, we, the receivers of the Torah, must believe and know that this world is a most honorable place for those who make proper use of it, and through it, a person merits the World to Come and the eternity of the soul…It was not in vain that the Rabbis stated, "Three days of weeping, seven for eulogy, thirty for [abstaining from] laundered garments and haircuts." If it were an inappropriate concept, they would not have designated three days for it. Similarly, we find that it is written regarding Avraham Avinu, "To eulogize Sarah and to weep for her," likewise regarding Yaakov, David HaMelech, and numerous others. See the introduction of the Ramban's Sefer Toras Ha'adam, and you will find sufficient response to this question. Nonetheless, it*

---

3   *Bereishis* 23:2.
4   Commentary to the Torah, *Devarim* 14:1.

is not appropriate to grieve excessively over a death, as stated clearly in the Gemara. Thus, I have written what appears to me in my humble opinion.[5]

The Torah commands us not to mourn excessively: "Do not gash yourselves, and do not create a bald spot between your eyes on account of a death."

The root of the mourning and grief over the passing of a loved one is twofold. First, there is the deep, sharp pain of the death itself, which hurts more than any other blow. In addition, there is the feeling of being orphaned and alone, the pain of longing for what was lost.

The two aforementioned explanations of the Rishonim correspond to these two aspects. Regarding the feelings of loneliness, the Torah states, "You are children to Hashem your God"; thus, even when a Jew loses his father or mother, he is not left alone. Hashem is our father, and we are His beloved children, and He stands over us and supports us, as David HaMelech says, "And I am always with You, You took hold of my right hand."[6]

And regarding the tragic, heartrending pain of the demise itself, the Torah states, "You are children to Hashem, your God," "And you shall know in your heart, that as a man chastises his son, so does Hashem your God chastise you."[7]

Whatever the situation, whatever the circumstance, we know that "all that Hashem does is for the best," and the Attribute of Justice is accompanied by mercy. Even when it appears to a person that he has been confronted with the Attribute of Justice, he must strengthen himself in his faith, and remind himself that when Hashem chastises him and brings him pain, it is only out of His love for him, a love greater than the love of a mother, and a compassion greater than the compassion of a father.

---

5   Sec. 3, 555 (985).
6   *Tehillim* 73:23.
7   *Devarim* 8:5.

TWELVE

Fortunate Are You, Rabbi Akiva

The great people of our nation, giants in Torah and fear of Heaven, risked their lives during times of religious persecution to teach Torah in public, to protect the flame from being extinguished. The following is related about Rabbi Akiva ben Yosef:

> The Rabbis taught: The wicked government [of Rome] once decreed that the Jews could not study Torah. Papus ben Yehudah found Rabbi Akiva gathering groups in public and studying Torah. He said to him, "Akiva, are you not afraid of the authorities?" He replied, "I will tell you a parable: To what may this be compared? To a fox walking along the riverbank who saw fish fleeing from place to place. It asked them, "From whom are you fleeing?" They replied, "From the traps with which people are hunting us." It said to them, "Would you like to come up on to the dry land and we will live together in the same way as our ancestors lived together?" They told it, "Are you the one who is called the wisest of animals? You are not wise, but a fool. If in the area where we are able to live, we are afraid, in a place where we would die, how much more so!" The same applies to us. Now we are sitting and studying Torah, about which it is written, "For it is your life and the lengthening of our days," yet this is

> the case [we are in danger]; were we to refrain from its study, how much more so." They said, it was not long before Rabbi Akiva was arrested and put in jail, and Papus ben Yehudah was also arrested and imprisoned together with him. He asked him, "Papus, what brought you here?" He replied, "Fortunate are you, Rabbi Akiva, that you were arrested on account of Torah; woe is to Papus, who was arrested for trivial matters."[1]

Who was Papus who conversed with Rabbi Akiva, and what were the trivial matters for which the wicked Roman government arrested him?

The answer can be found in the words of the *Vilna Gaon* and *Toras Kohanim*.

The *Sefer Imrei Noam*,[2] from the teachings of the *Vilna Gaon*, states that Papus ben Yehudah was none other than Papus the brother of Lulianus, who were the martyrs of Lod.[3] This is also stated in the *Sifra* to *Parashas Bechukosai*: "'And I shall break the grandeur of your might'...these are the great ones who are the pride of Yisrael, such as Papus ben Yehudah and Lulianus of Alexandria."[4]

Thus, Papus ben Yehudah was the very same person as Papus the brother of Lulianus.

Why were Papus and Lulianus captured? There appear to be two explanations. *Rashi* in *Taanis* relates that the daughter of the king had been found murdered.[5] A rumor spread that the Jews killed her, and a decree was made against them. Papus and Lulianus came forward and falsely confessed that they were guilty of killing her in order to save the entire nation. They were executed and the Jewish People were saved. The *Yerushalmi* in *Sheviis* states that they sacrificed their lives when refusing to drink from a glass vessel that was colored (with an emblem of *avodah zarah*).[6] They did so because during times of religious

---

1 Berachos 61b.
2 Ibid.
3 Rashi, Taanis 18b; Bava Basra 10b.
4 2:5.
5 Ibid.
6 10b.

persecution, a person is obligated to give his life even to refrain from wearing a shoe strap in the manner of idolaters.

We see that Papus sacrificed his life in sanctification of Hashem's name, in an exalted and glorified way, either to save the entire nation from a decree of death or to stand in the breach during a time of religious persecution. In regard to those who act in this way Chazal say, "No person can stand in their place."[7]

Nonetheless, Papus said to Rabbi Akiva, "Fortunate are you, Rabbi Akiva, that you were captured on account of Torah. Woe is to Papus, who was arrested for **trivial matters**," for compared to the merit of teaching Torah, all other mitzvos are considered trivial, as the *Yerushalmi* teaches, "All the mitzvos are not worth even one word of Torah."[8]

This is utterly astounding!

This teaches us how great the merit is of those who learn and teach Torah, "Greater than the Heavens is Your kindness; no eye has seen it, God, apart from You."[9]

---

7   Bava Basra 10b.
8   Pe'ah 1:4, 4a.
9   Yeshayahu 64:3.

THIRTEEN

May It Be Your Will That You Cloak Yourself in Your Mercy

There is a well-known comment of the holy Rabbi Shimshon of Ostropoli on the *pasuk* in *Yeshayah*, "On account of your sins, your mother has been sent away."[1] When the Beis Hamikdash stood and the Kohanim served their duty and offered the sacrifices, Hashem, so to speak, stood and offered the sacrifices of the Jewish People in the Heavenly Beis Hamikdash. Once the Beis Hamikdash was destroyed, "the glory of Yisrael was cast down to the earth from the Heavens"—referring to the priestly garments that were made for honor and glory, which Hashem cast down, no longer finding favor in the pleasant aroma of the sacrifices. This is alluded to in the *pasuk*, "On account of your sins, your mother has been sent away," for the word "אמכם—your mother," is an acronym for the four priestly garments worn during service in the Beis Hamikdash: אבנט, מכנסים, כתנת, מצנפת—the belt, breeches, tunic, and turban.

Based on this comment, we can explain the prayer Rabbi Yochanan would utter after he concluded his regular order of prayers:

---

1 50:1.

Rabbi Yochanan, upon finishing [his prayers], would say as follows: "May it be Your will, Hashem our God, that You look at our disgrace and see our suffering, ותתלבש ברחמיך—and cloak Yourself with Your mercy, ותתכסה בעוזך—and cover Yourself with Your might, ותתעטף בחסידותיך—and robe Yourself with Your kindness, ותתאזר בחנינותך—and gird Yourself with Your graciousness, and may Your attributes of goodness and humility come before You.[2]

- "ותתלבש ברחמיך—Cloak Yourself with Your mercy." This refers to the tunic, regarding which the term *"levishah"* is used, as the *pasuk* states, "כתנת בד קודש ילבש—He shall robe himself in a fitted linen tunic that is holy."[3]
- "ותתכסה בעוזך—Cover Yourself with Your might." This alludes to the breeches, where the term *"kisuy"* is used, as the *pasuk* states, "לכסות בשר ערוה—To cover the skin of their nakedness."[4]
- "ותתעטף בחסידותיך—Cloak Yourself with Your kindness." This refers to the turban, for which the term *"ituf"* is appropriate, as Chazal state, "Ten things were said regarding a *kos shel* berachah, one of which is *ituf*."[5] This refers to covering the person's head, as explained by the Rishonim.
- "ותתאזר בחנינותך—Gird Yourself with Your graciousness." This alludes to the belt, regarding which the term *"eizor"* is used, as in the *pasuk*, "ואזור עור אזור במתניו—And gird a belt of leather around his waist."[6]

This was the supplication of Rabbi Yochanan—that Hashem reestablish the glory of the Jewish People from the dust of its exile, and cloak Himself with His mercy, cover Himself with His might, robe Himself with His kindness, gird Himself with His graciousness, and desire the

---

2 *Berachos* 16b.
3 *Vayikra* 16:4.
4 *Shemos* 28:42.
5 *Berachos* 51a.
6 *Melachim II* 1:8.

Beis Hamikdash once again, with the return of the Kohanim to their service, and Yisrael to their splendor.

I have since found that the Gaon Rabbi Yechiel Heller makes the very same observations as the above.[7]

---

[7] Responsa, *Amudei Ohr*, glosses to 122:13.

FOURTEEN

Remove the Evil of Your Ways

Haftarah for Shabbos Chazon

> The vision of Yeshayahu ben Amotz, which he saw regarding Yehudah and Yerushalayim.
>
> Yeshayahu 1:1

This vision is a harsh one, among the sternest of the portions of rebuke, established by Chazal to be the haftarah for the Shabbos before Tishah B'Av.

Let us contemplate the words of the *Navi* and understand what brought about this great wrath.

First of all, we should note that the words of rebuke primarily relate to matters of wealth and theft, the lack of compassion and mercy toward the poor and destitute, and the lack of assistance offered to them. The Navi does not rebuke the Jews about the sanctity of Shabbos or their purity of heart, but rather about interpersonal mitzvos.

> *Learn to be benevolent, seek justice, rectify that which is stolen, judge the orphan, champion the cause of the widow.*[1]
>
> *Your silver was dross, your wine was watered down.*[2]

Wickedness and robbery, perversion of law and justice—that was what sullied us.

Furthermore:

> *Your princes were wayward and were all accomplices of thieves, who loved bribery and pursued payments, they did not judge the orphan, and the cause of the widow did not come before them.*[3]

As long as the princes and judges—the leaders of the people—are upright, even if the people are wayward, there remains hope and promise, for sooner or later their leaders and judges will punish the wrongdoers, rebuke those straying after them, and **the king will maintain the land with justice.**

This is not the case when the very leaders of the people, its princes and judges, have perverted their ways, and the flame has fallen even among the mighty cedars; then all hope is lost, and their only remedy is to be cut down.

The *Ketzos Hachoshen* comments on the difference between the people of Sodom, who were annihilated, and the people of Givah in the episode of the *pilegesh*.[4] Both sinned in a similar manner with severe and wicked abuse of others, and both perverted their ways and corrupted their paths. If so, why was Sodom given a decree of annihilation, swallowed into the earth without a remnant, whereas the people of Givah were punished by a plague but nonetheless endured?

He explains that the people of Sodom legislated laws of wickedness and legalized their acts of evil and immorality. Not only did they corrupt

---

1 *Yeshayahu* 1:17.
2 Ibid. 1:22.
3 Ibid. 1:23.
4 *Shev Shmaitsa*, introduction.

their ways—they codified laws of perversion, which became the very legislation of Sodom and Amorah. As such, there was no hope for them.

That was not so regarding the people of the Givah. Although they were wicked and acted cruelly to others, their laws were just, and their statutes were upright. As long as a nation has fair laws and honest judges, there is hope that they will repent and mend their ways. They were therefore punished and received atonement for their sin.

Thus, at the time of the *churban*, the Navi rebukes the Jewish People and cries bitterly, "Your princes were wayward and were all accomplices of thieves, who loved bribery and pursued payments, they did not judge the orphan, and the cause of the widow did not come before them."

FIFTEEN

The Vision of Yeshayahu Ben Amotz I

On the Shabbos before Tishah B'Av, we read the haftarah of *Chazon Yeshayahu*, which contains harsh rebuke for the leaders of Yisrael, as well as its people. Let us examine the reason for this practice.

The *Rambam* in *Hilchos Taanis* states:

> There are days on which all of Yisrael fast because of the tragedies that occurred on them, to arouse the hearts and to open up the paths of teshuvah, and serve to remind us of our evil actions, and of the deeds of our fathers which were akin to our actions today, causing these tragedies to befall both them and ourselves. For by remembering these matters we will return to proper conduct, as the pasuk states (Vayikra 26:40), "And they shall confess their sin and the sin of their fathers."[1]

The *Chasam Sofer* infers from the *Rambam* that the theme of the four fast days is not mourning but *teshuvah*.[2] However, I have written elsewhere that in my humble opinion, it is clear that the four fasts relate to

---

1 5:2.
2 Responsa, *Orach Chaim* 108.

mourning.³ Many halachos are stated instructing us not to divert our thoughts from mourning on these days. Nonetheless, when we bring the destruction of our Beis Hamikdash to our attention and mourn over it, it is our responsibility to fix what went wrong and do *teshuvah*, as the *Rambam* writes, "Anyone who does not mourn as Chazal enacted is acting cruelly. Rather, he should be afraid and worry, and examine his actions and repent."⁴ These words are particularly applicable to mourning over Yerushalayim and the Beis Hamikdash, for Chazal have stated, "Any generation in which it was not rebuilt is considered to have destroyed it."⁵

This is astounding. Any generation that does not merit the rebuilding of the Beis Hamikdash bears responsibility for the *churban*. For we do not only mourn over the *churban* of the Beis Hamikdash thousands of years ago, but for the Beis Hamikdash that was not rebuilt in our time. We fast so as to open our hearts to the path of *teshuvah*, as expressed by the *Rambam*.

The *Maharsha* in *Bechoros* relates that the twenty-one days between the seventeenth of Tammuz and Tishah B'Av correspond to the twenty-one days between Rosh Hashanah and Hoshana Rabbah.⁶ Just as the days from Rosh Hashanah to Sukkos are days of judgment and auspicious days for atonement from sin, so are the days from the seventeenth of Tammuz until Tishah B'Av days of judgment, repentance, and atonement.

Based on this assertion, the *Maharsha* explains the episode in which the elders of Athens brought two eggs before Rabbi Yehoshua ben Chananiah, one black and one white. He writes that the two eggs allude to these two sets of twenty-one days, as it takes twenty-one days for an egg to be formed. The black egg alludes to the twenty-one days between the seventeenth of Tammuz and Tishah B'Av, for it is customary for mourners to dress in black. The white egg alludes to the twenty-one

---

3   *Minchas Asher, Mo'adim*, sec. 2, 36.
4   *Hilchos Taanis*, chap. 1.
5   *Yerushalmi, Yoma* 4b.
6   8b.

days of atonement during the month of Tishrei, alluding to the *pasuk*, "If your sins will be as scarlet, they shall become white as snow."[7]

These days are not just days of mourning, but of introspection, repentance, and correction of our deeds, for if we are considered to have destroyed the Beis Hamikdash, it is our responsibility to rebuild it.

Therefore, the custom was established to recite *Chazon Yeshayahu*, so that we should repent, and correct our ways.

---

7   *Yeshayahu* 1:18.

SIXTEEN

The Vision of Yeshayahu Ben Amotz II

The haftarah we read on the Shabbos before Tishah B'Av is the opening chapter of *Sefer Yeshayahu*, the entire theme of which is rebuke and consolation. It is read before Tishah B'Av, so that we should consider the causes of the *churban*, and the areas in which we must repent.

The mother of all sin, according to the Navi, is the complacency that comes with routine, and the lack of contemplation of our actions. "The ox knows its master, and the donkey the trough of its owner, but Yisrael does not know; My nation does not give thought."[1] If so, it is certainly appropriate that we carefully consider the words of the Navi in this chapter.

If we reflect upon the Navi's words, we will see that he does not rebuke the people about *mitzvos bein adam laMakom* (mitzvos between man and God), but about *mitzvos bein adam la'chaveiro* (interpersonal mitzvos). The Navi Yeshayahu ben Amotz roars like a lion and rebukes the nation about theft, withholding payment, bribery, and perversion of justice, and at the lack of mercy and compassion displayed by the nation and its leaders: "Your silver was dross, your wine was watered

---

1   *Yeshayahu* 1:3.

down. Your princes were wayward and were all accomplices of thieves, who loved bribery and pursued payments, they did not judge the orphan, and the cause of the widow did not come before them."[2]

The Navi concludes with the words, "Tzion will be redeemed with justice, and its captives through charity."[3] Justice and fairness, charity and kindness—these are the foundation blocks of the perfection of man and nation.

It is apparent from the *pesukim* that the people of that generation were particularly careful regarding *mitzvos bein adam laMakom*. They offered numerous sacrifices, as the Navi declares, "What need do I have for your numerous offerings, says Hashem, I have been satiated with burnt-offerings of rams and the fats of young sheep, and the blood of bulls and lambs I do not desire." They were scrupulous in the observance of Shabbos and Yom Tov, as it states, "They proclaim the convocations of Rosh Chodesh and Shabbos; I cannot bear their iniquity together with their assembly. I have hated your [days of] Rosh Chodesh and your festivals; they have been to Me as a burden, I have grown weary of bearing [them]."

They prayed abundantly, but the Navi tells them, "When you spread out your hands, I shall hide My eyes from You, even when you pray abundantly, I shall not listen; your hands are full of blood."

For Hashem does not desire Divine service when we do not lead our lives according to the dictates of righteousness and justice, fairness and compassion.

We can imagine that these words were said in our time—as if the Navi Yeshayahu were standing in the streets of the city, directing his words at us.

We are fortunate that a wonderful generation has arisen, of those who toil in Torah and are scrupulous in mitzvah observance. Yet there is still a lot of work to be done and much correction needed in the area of interpersonal mitzvos and character traits, particularly regarding upright conduct and financial matters. We should be ashamed when members

---

2   Ibid. 1:22–23.
3   Ibid. 1:27.

of our people, righteous and pious people, act perversely with regard to damaging neighbors, as we see in *beis din* on a daily basis. Those who study Torah are involved in disputes and arguments, humiliating one another, while those in public service pursue bribery and corruption, and we ignore the cries of widows and orphans.

If we would only correct our paths, cleave to the *middos* of Hashem, and go in His ways of mercy and compassion, we would thereby merit the eternal salvation and the rebuilding of the Beis Hamikdash, speedily in our days, *Amen.*

SEVENTEEN

In the Great Metropolis of Rome

We are approaching the bitter and mournful day of Tishah B'Av, the day on which the luminaries dimmed and a great darkness descended upon the world; the day on which the two *Batei Mikdash* were destroyed, and rivers of blood and tears covered the land.

Yet, our mouths are still full of praise of Hashem; we have faith that all He does is for the best. We truly believe that Hashem resides with us even in the depths of our sorrow and the darkness of our exile, and His abundant mercy and kindness accompany us during times of Divine concealment just as in times of Divine favor; both when the Heavenly kingdom is revealed, and when it is hidden.

This appears to be the meaning of Rabbi Yehoshua ben Levi's statement in the *Yerushalmi*: "Rabbi Yehoshua ben Levi said: If a person asks you, 'Where is your God?' tell him, 'In the great metropolis of Edom.'" (The Venice edition reads, "In the great metropolis of Rome.")[1]

During the darkest days of the Holocaust, the great Gaon, Rabbi Yissachar Shlomo Teichtal, *Hy"d*, described those who, with a bitter heart and broken spirit, asked "Where is our God?" "Why has He hidden

---

1   *Yerushalmi, Taanis* 1:1, 3a.

His face from us?" He writes that this was what the great Amora Rabbi Yehoshua ben Levi, who lived not long after the *churban*, referred to. He taught us that if a person asks, "Where is our God?" you should respond, "In the great metropolis of Rome." In the place of evil, the very epicenter of apparently profound Divine concealment—even there Hashem is found in His abundant mercy and kindness, and all that He does is for the best, in a way that is beyond our understanding.

The central part of *Kedushah* is the following two *pesukim*: (1) "Holy, holy, holy is Hashem, Lord of Hosts, the entire world is full of His glory," sourced in *Yeshayahu* 6:3; and (2) "Blessed is the glory of Hashem from His place," sourced in *Yechezkel* 3:12.

In *Maseches Chagigah* 13b, Chazal state:

> *Rava said: All that Yechezkel saw, Yeshayahu saw. To what may Yechezkel be compared? To a villager who saw the king. And to what may Yeshayahu be compared? To a city-dweller who saw the king.*
>
> *Rashi explains: "Yeshayahu saw"—when Divine inspiration dwelled upon him, as the pasuk states (Yeshayahu 6), "And I saw Hashem sitting on a high and exalted throne," he did not see fit to relate all that he saw, for he was a prince and grew up in the palace, and just like a city-dweller who sees the king is not astounded and is not in awe, and does not see fit to relate everything...*

Were I not afraid to suggest it, I would add another dimension. These two prophets prophesized in different eras and under different circumstances.

The Navi Yeshayahu prophesized when the Beis Hamikdash stood, and the glory of Hashem filled the *Heichal*. In his vision, he saw ministering angels sanctifying His Great name, proclaiming Holiness to the Holy and Awesome One, and indeed, **"The entire world is full of His glory!"**

The Navi Yechezkel, however, prophesized by the river, already within the suffering and affliction of the Babylonian exile, when Divine concealment prevailed. In his vision he saw a stormy wind, a thick cloud, and a searing fire. Through his prophetic spirit, he saw an awesome vision, full of fear and dread, but from within all the darkness and thick cloud, he saw "radiance surrounded it, and the appearance of pure flame from within the fire," and he thus proclaimed, "Blessed is the glory of Hashem from His place." **"From His place"**—even though we have not merited that "the entire world is full of His glory," for concealment had covered the revelation—"the hidden God is concealed in His pavilion."

In the *Kedushah*, the Jewish People pair the prophecy of revelation of Yeshayahu with the prophecy of concealment of Yechezkel, for in reality, there is no difference between the two, just in their external appearance.

Understanding in Hindsight

And you shall see My back, but My face you shall not see.[2]

In his introduction to *Sh'eilos U'Teshuvos Kol Aryeh*, the author cites a novel and profound explanation of this *pasuk* from his great *rebbi*, the *Chasam Sofer*. Moshe yearned to understand the ways of Hashem to the full extent of Divine providence. Hashem told him, "And you shall see My back," referring to the perspective of hindsight, the retrospective understanding of what Hashem has done. However, "My face, you shall not see"—understanding the ways of Hashem while they are being implemented is hidden from man—even Moshe did not merit the level of "seeing His face."

With this in mind, the *Kol Aryeh* goes on to explain the comments of *Rashi*: "'And you shall see My back'—this refers to the knot of the tefillin." The [essence] of the mitzvah of tefillin is the paragraphs of *k'rias Shema*. In the first *pasuk* of *Shema* we recite, "**Hashem Elokeinu Hashem Echad—Hashem our God, Hashem is One.**" The name "Hashem" refers to the Attribute of Mercy and the name "Elokim" to the Attribute of Justice. This is the meaning of our proclamation. Although we sometimes perceive the Attribute of Mercy and at other times the Attribute of Justice, we know that all Hashem does is for the best, and

---

2   *Shemos* 33:23.

even the Attribute of Justice is essentially mercy. Thus we declare, "*Hashem Elokeinu Hashem Echad.*"

The *Kol Aryeh* adds that the two straps that emerge from the head tefillin, one to the right and one to the left, allude respectively to the Attribute of Mercy, which is represented by the right side, and the Attribute of Justice, which is represented by the left side, as the Gemara states, "One should always push away with the left hand but draw close with the right hand."[3] The knot of the tefillin ties Justice and Mercy together and teaches us that the two Attributes are one and the same—the Attribute of Justice is also Mercy. This is truly a beautiful interpretation!

The Gemara in *Berachos* relates, "Moshe wished to understand why the wicked prosper and the righteous suffer."[4] Rabbi Meir and Rabbi Yosi argue as to whether Moshe was given an answer or not.

It seems to me that Moshe, our faithful shepherd, was asking this question not just about Divine conduct toward righteous and wicked individuals, but also about the history of the Jewish nation. The Jews are cherished as the children of Hashem, and nobody among the other nations, be they righteous in their ways and pious in their actions, can compare to the people of Hashem who cleave to His Torah and faith. Yet, no other nation is as afflicted and persecuted, exile after exile, banished and cast away. Already now, having just left Egypt with open revelation of the Shechinah, with drums and dancing, "While the King was still at the banquet, my perfume lost its scent"—due to the sin of the golden calf, they encountered death and destruction.

This was Moshe's question: "The righteous suffer while the wicked prosper"—the wicked nations sit in tranquility and calm, every city built up and established, while the city of God remains in ruins, and the Nation of Hashem is degraded and despised.

Hashem told Moshe, "And you shall see My back," and showed him the knot of the tefillin connecting the right and the left, Justice and Mercy. Hashem thus alluded to him that even if he could not understand this

---

3   *Sotah* 47b.
4   7a.

matter—the secrets of Divine conduct—he needed to know that all Hashem does is for the best, and even the Attribute of Justice is in fact nothing but kindness.

"A Decree before Me"

Chazal relate that Hashem showed Moshe the Torah of Rabbi Akiva and Moshe requested, "You have shown me his Torah, show me his reward."[5] Hashem replied, "Moshe, turn **backward**," and showed him the death of Rabbi Akiva, and his flesh being sold in the market. When Moshe Rabbeinu cried out, "This is Torah and this is its reward?!" Hashem told him, "It is a decree from **before Me**."

In light of the above, it appears that Hashem was telling him, "Turn **backward**, it is a decree from **before Me**"—for I have already told you that "You shall see **My back**, but **My face** you shall not see," and this decree can only be understood with the perspective of **forward**, not with the view of "you shall see **My back**." This is the meaning of "Turn **backward**…it is a decree from **before Me**."

A Place Called Mistarim

And if you will not listen to this, in hidden places I shall weep.[6]

When Hashem wanted to destroy the Beis Hamikdash, He said, "As long as I am inside it, the nations of the world will not be able to touch it. Rather, I shall shield My eyes from it, and I shall swear that I shall not engage with it until the time of the End [i.e., the Final Redemption], and enemies shall come and destroy it." Immediately, Hashem swore with His right hand and turned backward, as the pasuk states (Eichah 2:3), "He has turned His right hand away before the enemy," and at that time, the enemies entered the Sanctuary and burned it. Once it was burned, Hashem said, "I no longer have a place of residence in the land, I shall remove My presence from it and

---

5   *Menachos* 29b.
6   *Yirmiyahu* 13:17.

arise to My first abode," as the pasuk states (Hoshea 5:15), "I shall go and return to My place, until they admit their guilt and seek My face." At that time, Hashem was weeping and said, "Woe is to Me, what have I done, I rested My presence in the lower realms because of Yisrael and now that they have sinned, I have returned to My previous abode, chas v'shalom, I have been a laughingstock for the nations and a mockery for creation." At that time, Matat-ron came and fell on his face, and said before Him, "Master of the World, let me cry and You will not cry." He told him, "If you do not let Me cry now, I shall go to a place to which you do not have permission to enter and cry there," as the pasuk states (Yirmiyahu 13:17), "And if you shall not listen to this, in hidden places I shall weep."[7]

How astounding are these words! It is not the Navi saying that he would cry in hidden places, but Hashem Himself, "I shall go to a place to which you do not have permission to enter, and cry there."

We find a similar theme in *Chagigah*, where the Gemara asks, "But is there a concept of Hashem weeping? Surely Rav Papa said, there is no sadness before Hashem…There is no contradiction: one [statement] refers to [weeping] in private, and the other refers to [weeping] in public."[8]

When Hashem destroyed the Beis Hamikdash and when Yisrael are in pain and mourning, Hashem also cries. And although there is no sadness before Hashem, as the *pasuk* states, "Gladness and joy in His place,"[9] nonetheless, it is different when it is in private, for "Hashem has a place that is called *Mistarim*," and there, even Hashem, so to speak, sheds tears and cries.

The depth of this idea appears to be that while "All Hashem does is for the best,"[10] and even the Attribute of Justice is inherently merciful, nonetheless, the Jewish People had been exiled from their land, their blood was spilled like water, and the sacrifices and song ceased. And

---

7   Eichah Rabbah, Pesichta.
8   5b.
9   Divrei Hayamim 1 16:27.
10 Berachos 60b.

when the Jewish People are in pain, "The Shechinah, what utterance does it say? My head is in pain, My arms are in pain."[11] Hashem, so to speak, goes to a place into which no other creation has permission to enter, not even the angel Matat-ron. This place is called *Mistarim*, and there even Hashem cries.

Lest we think this is merely a place called *Mistarim*; not only can no creation enter there, and no eye can see it, but no mind can comprehend it,[12] and no man understands its ways.

This place called *Mistarim* is none other than a reflection of the Divine pronouncement, "It is a decree from before Me," regarding which it is stated, "And My face, you shall not see."

May we merit soon to reach the time when we will be able to look back and recite *Hatov V'Hameitiv* on all that we have experienced, when gladness and joy will fill all places.

---

11 *Sanhedrin* 46a.
12 Introduction to *Tikkunei Zohar* 17a.

EIGHTEEN

This Storm Is Because of Me

We are standing on the eve of this bitter and mournful day, the Ninth of Av, and it is our duty not only to mourn, but also to give thought, to examine our actions and deeds, and to repent. For Chazal have stated, "Any generation in which the Beis Hamikdash was not rebuilt, **is considered to have destroyed it.**"[1]

Not only is it considered that **it was destroyed in their time** (as is commonly assumed), but it is considered that **they have destroyed it**. And if we are meant to feel that we were the ones who destroyed the Beis Hamikdash, we most certainly have a responsibility to examine our deeds and to put right the evil of our actions.

The terminology used by Chazal is, "It is considered as if **they** had destroyed it." It is very easy to point the blame at others and to exclude oneself. We tend to do this on a regular basis—to view the faults of others and to place the blame of the generation's faults on them, while only seeing our own virtues. However, this is not the way of the Torah. When a wave arose that threatened to sink his ship, Yonah HaNavi stood up and declared, **"This storm is because of me!"** Yonah, a righteous and holy prophet of Hashem, found himself on a ship with a group of

---

1   *Yerushalmi, Yoma* 5a.

gentiles, compared with whom he was a thousand times more sanctified and exalted—yet he knew that the storm was because of him.

The Gemara in *Gittin* relates:

> The Rabbis taught: Rabbi Yehoshua ben Chanania once went to the great metropolis of Rome. They informed him, "There is a child imprisoned, with beautiful eyes and fine appearance, whose hair is arranged into curls." He went and stood at the entrance of the prison and announced, "Who has given over Yaakov to be plundered, and Yisrael to looters?" The lad answered, "Surely this is Hashem toward Whom we have sinned, and they did not desire to follow in His paths, and they did not listen to His Torah." He declared, "I am sure that he will become an authority of halachah in Yisrael. I am not leaving until I redeem him with whatever sum they demand." It is said, he did not leave until he redeemed him with a large sum of money, and it was not long until he became an authority of halachah in Yisrael, and who was he? Rabbi Yishmael ben Elisha.[2]

The question arises: What did Rabbi Yehoshua ben Chanania see in the words of the young boy that so inspired him? What spark of greatness did he hear in his answer that made him sure that he would become a halachic authority and a leader of the Jewish People?

The answer may be detected upon close examination of the *pasuk* quoted. For it seems to contain an inherent contradiction. First it states, "Surely this is Hashem toward Whom **we** have sinned"—it is we who have sinned. But it then states, "**They** did not desire to follow in His paths to walk upon, and **they** did not listen to His Torah"—it was others who did not desire to follow in Hashem's paths or listen to His Torah.

The Navi implies that during times of punishment, when we are admonished and chastised, we must first consider our own deeds before pointing our finger at others and blaming them. It is always easier to

---

2   58a.

blame others and to consider them culpable for our misfortune than to consider our own actions and examine ourselves for wrongdoing. How easy would it have been for this child to point the blame at others during those times of wicked decrees, to find them at fault and hold them culpable! On the one hand, there was the wicked Roman kingdom; on the other hand, the *Tzedukim* and *Baytusim*, who reared their heads to uproot the Oral Torah—and in the middle the *Biryonim*, the reckless ones, who cast off the yoke of the Sages and brought tragedy to the entire nation.

Yet he did not do so. **Surely, this is Hashem toward whom we have sinned**. This storm is because of us! We have sinned and we must repent. Only then did he continue, "**They** did not desire to follow in His ways and **they** did not listen to His Torah."

This is conduct of greatness! Greatness of soul and spirit, which is the conduct of the leaders of the Jewish People. This is the path we learn from Chazal who rebuke us and chastise us when they discuss the *churban*. It was due to our sins that the Beis Hamikdash was destroyed and the Jewish People were exiled from their land!

Upon hearing this response, Rabbi Yehoshua declared, "I am sure that he will be an authority of halachah in the Jewish People!"

The Message for Our Times

Chazal state that the First Beis Hamikdash was destroyed due to the three cardinal sins: idolatry, adultery, and murder.[3] However, at the time of the second *churban*, the people toiled in Torah and were scrupulous in their mitzvah observance. Nevertheless, the Beis Hamikdash was destroyed due to the sin of baseless hatred. This teaches us that baseless hatred is equal to the three most severe transgressions in the Torah!

Likewise, in our generation, many feel that they know with certainty why the Beis Hamikdash has not yet been rebuilt, who is holding it back, and on whose account is this storm. The reform, conservatives,

---

3   *Yoma* 9b; *Yerushalmi, Yoma* 4b.

secularists, assimilated marriages, etc., The list goes on, but is based on a fundamental mistake. **This storm is because of us!**

It is not due to the sin of those who were born into irreligious homes, not on account of those who have excluded themselves from the congregation and strayed to graze in foreign pastures, but because of us. We are *b'nei Torah* and are fortunate to be infused with the light of Torah. The words of Torah and Chazal are clear to us and are fluent in our mouths. We know the truth, yet we do not always follow in its light, preaching well but not practicing likewise. This storm is because of us. It is concerning us that Chazal asserted, "It is considered that they destroyed it."

Let us examine our actions, strengthen ourselves in Torah study, in loving our fellow, in proper intent during prayer, and good character traits, and we will thereby merit that Hashem will have mercy on us, and build the Beis Hamikdash speedily in our days.

NINETEEN

She Has Become Like a Widow

> *"She has become like a widow."*
> *Rav Yehudah said in the name of Rav:*
> *Like a widow, but not an actual widow;*
> *like a woman whose husband has traveled*
> *to a distant land, but plans to return to her.*
> Sanhedrin 104a

We are taught by Yirmiyahu HaNavi that even during the exile, the Jewish People are not widowed, but are rather akin to a widow. They are likened to a woman whose husband has traveled overseas—one longing for her husband in a distant land—whose husband also misses his faithful and beloved wife who remains alone in her house, her soul yearning for him.

And from his distant land the husband vows in his heart that when he finally returns home and his exile comes to an end, he will honor his wife and bestow bounty and blessing upon her, corresponding to all the days of her poverty and suffering.

Similarly, when the Jewish People were exiled and the Shechinah departed from them, it was not a complete separation like death or divorce, but akin to a woman whose husband has traveled overseas. The Jewish People yearn for the presence of His Holiness, and Hashem desires to dwell among them. And when He wills it and fulfills the request of our hearts, "Gladden us like the days of our affliction"—He will bestow unparalleled bounty and blessing upon us.

In addition, all those who extended kindness toward the Jewish People will receive their reward, for if a husband travels abroad, and a person sustains his wife, the husband must reimburse him.[1]

May it be Hashem's will that we soon merit that He will return to His people—"and may our eyes witness Your return to Tzion with compassion."[2]

---

1   *Kesubos* 107b.
2   *Shemoneh Esreh*.

TWENTY

They Started to Weep, but Rabbi Akiva Laughed

On another occasion, they ascended to Yerushalayim. When they arrived at Mount Scopus, they rent their clothing. Once they arrived at the Temple Mount, they saw a fox emerge from the Holy of Holies. They started to weep but Rabbi Akiva started to laugh. They asked him, "Why are you laughing?" He replied, "Why are you crying?" They told him, "The place about which it is written, 'The stranger who draws near shall die' and now foxes are walking there, should we not weep?" He replied, "That is why I am laughing. For it is written, 'And I shall appoint for myself faithful witnesses, Uriah HaKohen and Zechariah ben Yevorachyahu.' Now, what connection does Uriah have to Zechariah? Uriah lived in the period of the First Beis Hamikdash, and Zechariah lived in the period of the Second Beis Hamikdash? Rather, the verse links the prophecy of Uriah to the prophecy of Zechariah. In [the prophecy of] Uriah, it is stated, 'Therefore, on account of you, Tzion will be plowed over like a field,' and in [the prophecy of] Zechariah it is stated, 'Elderly men and women will once again sit in the streets of Yerushalayim.' Until the prophecy of Uriah was fulfilled, I was afraid that the prophecy of Zechariah would not be fulfilled.

Now that the prophecy of Uriah has been fulfilled, I know that the prophecy of Zechariah will be fulfilled." With these words, they told him, "Akiva, you have comforted us, Akiva, you have comforted us."[1]

There appears to be a striking question on the words of Rabbi Akiva, "Until the prophecy of Uriah was fulfilled, I was afraid that the prophecy of Zechariah would not be fulfilled." May one doubt one prophecy because one has not seen another prophecy being fulfilled? Further, did Rabbi Akiva not know that the Beis Hamikdash had been destroyed, the Sanctuary burned, and Tzion plowed over until he saw a fox exiting the Holy of Holies? If so, why was he laughing?

The *Maharal* of Prague explains that the grandeur and glory of the redemption is always proportional to the severity of the exile that preceded it.[2] The harsher the exile, the more glorified the redemption will be, for "absence is the cause of existence." This is why the First Beis Hamikdash was greater than the Second; since the Egyptian exile was longer and harsher than the Babylonian exile, it was therefore appropriate that the First Beis Hamikdash be greater and more glorious than the second.

In this light, the *Maharal* explains the words of Rabbi Akiva. He witnessed how harsh and terrible the decree of the *churban* was, for the place about which it is stated, "The stranger who approaches shall die," namely, the Holy of Holies where even angels were unable to enter[3]—its glory was now lowered to the dust, and foxes walked there. When he saw this, he drew a parallel in his heart as to how exulted and glorious the redemption would be.

Rabbi Akiva saw the light within the darkness, the mercy within the justice. His colleagues were weeping because of the prophecy of Uriah, yet he was laughing because of the prophecy of Zechariah, for exile is only the key to redemption. From within the darkness of the exile, the

---

1   *Makkos* 24b.
2   *Netzach Yisrael* 26.
3   *Yerushalmi, Yoma* 27a, and *Sukkah* 21b.

light of redemption bursts forth, and the darkness of the night breaks into the dawn of Mashiach.

The Birth Pangs of Mashiach

On the bitter and mournful day of Tishah B'Av, we sit on the floor, mourning and downcast, lamenting the destruction of the Beis Hamikdash and the burning of the Sanctuary. However, the custom is that the final *kinnah* is recited standing. After sitting on the floor, we arise and recite, "Weep O Zion and its cities, like a woman in her birth pangs." We compare the suffering of the *churban* to the pain of a woman in childbirth. Though childbirth is a source of great suffering, pain, and agony, the woman giving birth knows that from the depths of her suffering, new life is born. She is aware that "With pain you shall beget children,"[4] yet she lovingly accepts the pain of childbirth to merit a child, and to hold a baby in her arms.

Likewise, the sufferings of the *churban* are the birth pangs of the redemption of Yisrael and eternal salvation. From the darkness of exile, the light of redemption sparks forth, for the travails preceding Mashiach are the birth pangs of the redemption of Yisrael.

"May it be Your will that the Beis Hamikdash be rebuilt speedily in our days, and grant us our portion in Your Torah, and there we will serve You with awe, like days of old and in years gone by."[5]

---

4   *Bereishis* 3:16.
5   *Shemoneh Esreh.*

TWENTY-ONE

The Keruvim Were Embracing One Another

> *Reish Lakish said: When the gentiles entered the Sanctuary, they saw the Keruvim (Cherubim) embracing one another. They took them out to the marketplace and said, "These Jews, whose blessing is a blessing and whose curse is a curse, involve themselves in these matters?" Immediately, they mocked them as it states, "All those who honored her turned to mock her for they saw her nakedness."*
>
> Yoma 54b

This statement of Chazal is very puzzling. In *Maseches Bava Basra* it states that when the Jewish People were fulfilling the will of Hashem, the faces of the *Keruvim* would turn toward one another, but when they were not fulfilling the will of Hashem, they would face the walls of the Sanctuary.[1] The time of the *churban* was surely a period in which the Jewish People were not fulfilling the will of Hashem. Yet, not only were the *Keruvim* facing one another, they were

---

1   99a.

embracing with absolute love, which had never occurred before. This question is already raised by the *Ritva* and *Maharsha*.

The *B'nei Yissaschar*[2] cites the Maggid of Mezritch, who explains that specifically at the time of the *churban*, the Attribute of Love was empowered against the Attribute of Justice, in line with the halachah, "A man is obligated to remember his wife [with intimacy] before leaving on a journey."[3] Thus, at the time of the *churban* and the decree of exile, the *Keruvim* were embracing one another, alluding to the love Hashem has for the Jewish People.[4]

We may add that in light of the *pasuk*, "And you shall know in your heart that in the manner in which a man chastises his son, Hashem your God chastises you,"[5] when a father rebukes his child and strikes him, his heart is broken and torn inside. Specifically, when he must strike his son, his compassion is aroused. Thus, when our Father in Heaven chastises us, His Attribute of Love is intensified.

Man's conduct also reflects Divine conduct in this regard. The most righteous of our people reached their greatest spiritual heights specifically when they gave their lives in sanctification of Hashem's name during times of persecution. The Gemara relates how Rabbi Akiva accepted the yoke of Heaven upon himself while his flesh was being torn apart with iron combs.[6] In fact, the *Yerushalmi* adds that during this awesome moment of justice, as his flesh was torn with iron combs, **he was laughing**.[7] Rabbi Chanina ben Teradyon similarly sanctified Hashem's name in an awesome fashion as he was burned alive. This has likewise been the reaction of pure and holy martyrs in every generation.

With great love, Hashem chastises us, and with great love, His pious ones accept upon themselves the Attribute of Justice.

---

2   Tammuz-Av, *maamar* 3.
3   Yevamos 62b.
4   See the full text of the *B'nei Yissaschar*, where in light of the above, he offers a beautiful explanation of the Midrash that Mashiach ben David is born on Tishah B'Av (*Esther Rabbah*, *Pesichta* 11).
5   Devarim 8:5.
6   Berachos 61b.
7   Ibid. 67b.

TWENTY-TWO

Grant Our Portion in Your Torah

May it be Your will, Hashem our God and the God of our fathers, that the Beis Hamikdash be rebuilt speedily in our days, and grant our portion in Your Torah, and there we shall serve You with fear, as in days of old and previous years.

Avos 5:20

The *minhag* is to conclude the *Amidah* with this prayer, as stated by the Rama.[1] It is thus certainly appropriate to contemplate its significance.

At first glance, the sequence of this *tefillah* seems strange. What is the connection between the supplication, "Grant our portion in Your Torah," and the beginning of the prayer, "May the Beis Hamikdash be rebuilt speedily in our days"? They appear to be two separate supplications.

---

1   *Orach Chaim* 123:1.

The explanation that is commonly offered is that until the Divine will is aroused to return His presence to Yerushalayim, we are left with the miniature *Batei Mikdash*—the shuls and *batei midrash*—and when a person sits and studies Torah, even alone, the Shechinah resides with him. When the Beis Hamikdash was destroyed, Rabbi Yochanan ben Zakkai requested, "Give me Yavneh and its elders,"[2] for he realized that after the *churban*, the entire future of the Jewish People depended on the study of Torah and the scholars of Yavneh. For this reason, Rabbi Akiva gave his life at the time of the *churban* to spread Torah,[3] as did Rabbi Chanina ben Teradyon.[4] Thus, the meaning of the requests in the *tefillah* above is that we begin by asking for the rebuilding of the Beis Hamikdash, and then say that until that time, "Grant our portion in Your Torah, and we will thereby merit the presence of the Shechinah in our exile."

I have heard another explanation, based on the following statement of Chazal: "One who studies the laws of the *Olah*-offering, it is as though he offered an *Olah*. One who studies the laws of the *Chatas*-offering, it is as though he offered a *Chatas*."[5]

In other words, we ask Hashem to grant us our portion in Torah—meaning the Torah of the offerings—and thus it is as though we serve Him in the Beis Hamikdash.

However, these explanations do not sit well with the simple understanding of this prayer, for it continues, "And there we shall serve You with fear, as in days of old…" implying that the entire prayer refers to a time when the Beis Hamikdash will indeed be rebuilt.

We may suggest the following. There is a common misconception that when the Beis Hamikdash was destroyed, we lost the pillar of *avodah*, for the *korbanos* were discontinued, the lights of the *Menorah* were extinguished, and Mount Tzion was laid desolate and overrun by foxes, but it is assumed that the pillar of Torah remained untouched. However,

---

2   *Gittin* 56b.
3   *Berachos* 62a.
4   *Avodah Zarah* 18a.
5   *Menachos* 110a.

this is not the case. Just as the *avodah* was discontinued, so was the clarity in Torah and wisdom vastly diminished.

These are the words of our master the *Vilna Gaon*, in his introduction to *Tikkunei Zohar*, in explanation of the *pasuk* in *Megillas Eichah*, "Her kings and princes are among the nations, **there is no Torah**":[6]

> The concept here is similar to that expressed by the *pasuk*, "For He had not brought rain…and there was no man." For man is the *tzaddik* to water the ground, whether via rain, or through rivers from which he makes channels. When man is diligent and successful in his work, he waters them, but if he does not do so, the land drinks from that which earlier ones watered and left over. Likewise, regarding the *tzaddik* above, **and likewise regarding Torah; for now, we receive nothing new from the Torah as they did during the time of the Beis Hamikdash, only what we find in the writings of the earlier Sages. When the Beis Hamikdash stood, they would "water" the Torah**, as is written with regard to Rabbi Akiva; that matters that were not revealed to Moshe Rabbeinu were revealed to him…and he would expound on every crown [of every letter in the Sefer Torah]—and that is the watering of the Torah. This is not the case now that "Her kings and princes…there is no Torah," and all we have is that which develops from the teachings of the earlier Sages, endeavoring to understand their words.

The *Gaon* also expresses this concept in his commentary to *Avos*,[7] on the words, "May it be Your will, Hashem our God, that that You rebuild the Beis Hamikdash speedily in our days, and grant our portion in Your Torah." The *Gaon* notes that the correct position of this statement is at the end of the chapter,[8] regarding the teaching of Ben Hei Hei that reward is proportional to the pain involved, where he comments:

---

6 2:9.
7 5:23.
8 Mishnah 23.

> As it is written (Mishlei 14), "From every toil, there shall be gain." And it is here that it should state, "May it be Your will that the Beis Hamikdash be rebuilt...," similar to the end of [Maseches] Tamid. Here, because it deals with the general theme of Torah, "Moshe received the Torah...," **and there is no Torah without the Beis Hamikdash**, as it is stated (Eichah 2:9), "Her kings and her princes are among the nations, there is no Torah," it therefore states [at the conclusion of the maseches], "May it be Your will that the Beis Hamikdash be rebuilt...," as it is stated (Yeshayahu 11:9), "And the land shall be filled with the knowledge of Hashem."

The *Gaon* writes similarly in his commentary to *Shir Hashirim* that of the three pillars of the world, namely, Torah, *avodah* (Divine service) and *gemilus chassadim* (acts of kindness), the only one that remains after the *churban* is *chessed*.[9]

We see from his words that after the *churban*, the wellsprings of wisdom were stopped up and the fountain of Torah no longer springs forth. All we can do is review and sharpen that which the mighty Torah scholars left us as an inheritance, from the times that Divine inspiration resided on them in the *Lishkas Hagazis*.

The *Chasam Sofer* writes:

> It is known that from the day we were exiled from our land, the Divine channels of blessing were impaired, and people run after their livelihood but do not attain it; and even after great toil, the flavor of fruits were reduced, and there is no blessing in the gathered produce, as we elaborate in the piyut in the Mussaf of Yom Kippur. More than this, however, is the loss of the founts of wisdom—which used to flow in Yisrael—which were blocked, for the air of Eretz Yisrael brings wisdom (Bava Basra 158a), and the Shechinah would reside there. [Furthermore, we have lost the sources of wisdom about which it is stated:] Why was

---

9   6:4.

> it called Mount Moriah, for halachic rulings ("horaah") were issued from there to all Yisrael (Taanis 16a), and it was called the Simchas Beis HaShoeivah, for they drew ("shaavu") Divine inspiration (Bereishis Rabbah 9). One day of Torah study in Eretz Yisrael during that time of spiritual connection was worth more than a thousand days today, and they would attain in a short period what we do not attain in our entire lives on our land.[10]

The *Chasam Sofer* expresses the very same theme as the *Vilna Gaon*—that after the *churban*, the founts of Torah and wisdom were blocked up, and the light of Torah was dimmed.

In light of this, we can also answer the question posed by the *Kesef Mishneh*,[11] who asks why the Amora'im were unable to argue with the Tanna'im.[12]

In light of the above, it appears that since the Tanna'im merited to sit in the *Lishkas Hagazis* and were endowed with Divine inspiration as the Shechinah resided in their *beis midrash*, their students after them merited to draw from the wellsprings of their Torah. The period of the Amora'im, however, was initiated in darkness, only beginning after the *churban*, when the clarity of vision had already been dimmed. They were thus unable to argue with the Tanna'im.

Let us examine the words of the *Rambam*:

> The Beis Din Hagadol in Yerushalayim are the mainstay of Torah She'baal Peh; they are the pillar of halachic authority, and from them, law and judgment issues forth to all Yisrael, and the Torah confirms regarding them, "According to the Torah that they shall teach you, and the law that they dictate to you, you shall follow."[13]

---

10 *D'rashos* 3, *D'rush* for *Rosh Hashanah*, p. 18.
11 *Hilchos Mamrim* 2:1.
12 See *Minchas Asher, Devarim* 26.
13 *Hilchos Mamrim* 1:1.

We see that the *Beis Din Hagadol*, which sat in the *Lishkas Hagazis*, in the place of the Shechinah, and which was endowed with Divine inspiration, was the "mainstay of *Torah She'baal Peh*," and the halachic pillar of authority to the entire Jewish People.

However, we can make a further inference from the *Rambam's* words, **"The Torah assures** regarding them…that which they dictate to you, you shall follow…." We might ask, what assurance is given here? Surely, there is only a commandment and warning! It seems that not only is it a mitzvah to listen to the *Beis Din Hagadol*, there is also an assurance that the Shechinah is with them, and the halachah follows them in every case, as if the Shechinah is speaking from their throats. For it is stated that all of Yisrael are commanded to accept their rulings, and whoever argues with them is considered a *zaken mamrei* (rebellious sage).

It also appears that this is why, since the *churban*, we no longer judge cases of capital punishment. For even though the matter is a *gezeiras ha'kasuv* (a command from Hashem), nevertheless, we can suggest a reason for it. Only while the *Beis Din Hagadol* was present, and the pillar of halachic authority resided in the place of the Shechinah—and the Torah of truth was in their mouths and issued forth from there to the entire world—was it possible to judge cases of capital punishment. However, after the *churban*, once the clarity of vision was diminished, the mainstay of *Torah She'baal Peh* was weakened and doubts amassed in Yisrael, it was no longer possible to judge cases of capital punishment, for when there is the slightest level of doubt we may not cause the loss of a Jewish life.

As long as the Beis Hamikdash stood in its splendor, with the Kohanim at their service, the Leviim at their platform, and the great ones of Yisrael and the heads of the Great Sanhedrin with their Torah, the Beis Hamikdash was the center of Torah and *avodah* for the Jewish nation, and any important or difficult matter that arose throughout the world was brought there.[14] That was what established the Torah of truth and conduct of truth to the Jewish People.

---

14 *Griz Al HaTorah, Beshalach.*

That is the meaning of our supplication that the Beis Hamikdash be rebuilt speedily in our days. Then we will merit that on the one hand, "our portion be in Your Torah," and on the other, that "there we shall serve You with fear like days of old," and the Torah and *avodah* shall return to us with all their glory and splendor.

"May it be Your will, Hashem our God and the God of our fathers, that the Beis Hamikdash be rebuilt speedily in our days, and grant our portion in Your Torah, and there we shall serve You with fear, as in days of old and previous years. And may the offering of Yehudah and Yerushalayim be pleasing to Hashem, as in days of old and previous years."

TWENTY-THREE

Do Not Revoke Your Covenant with Us

> *When was Megillas Kinnos [Eichah] composed? Rabbi Yehudah said: In the days of Yehoyakim. Rabbi Nechemiah responded: Does one weep over a dead person before he has died? Rather, when was it said? After the churban—and [the verse] is interpreted as, "How she has sat alone" [in the past tense].*
>
> Eichah Rabbah 1:1

In *Maseches Bava Basra*, the Gemara states that the author of *Megillas Eichah* was Yirmiyahu, but it does not discuss when he wrote it.[1] This is discussed in the Midrash quoted above. Rabbi Yehudah contends that it was written in the days of Yehoyakim, which was many years before the *churban*. Rabbi Nechemiah finds this a difficult contention—does one cry over a deceased person before they

---

1 14b.

have passed away? Rather, the *Megillah* must have been written after the *churban*.

Rabbi Yehudah appears to hold that indeed, it is appropriate to cry over a deceased person before they have died. The prophet declares, "Rend your hearts and not your clothing."[2] Had the Jewish People cried over their dead before their demise—had they rent their hearts in repentance, prayer, and charity—they would not have needed to rend their clothing in mourning over their actual dead, for Hashem would have forgiven them, as it states, "For I do not desire the death of the deceased, rather that he should repent from his ways and live."[3]

According to Rabbi Yehudah, *Eichah* is not a lament over past events, but a *Megillah* of rebuke. The Navi described the *churban* before it occurred so that the Jewish People would take heart to fully repent, and to better their ways and paths.

This lesson applies to all generations. Chazal state, "Any generation in which the Beis Hamikdash is not rebuilt, is considered to have destroyed it."[4] Therefore, in every generation and every year, when the days of mourning approach, we are commanded to examine our deeds and repent.

Let us take note of the words of the *Rambam* in *Hilchos Taanis*:

> *There are days on which all of Yisrael fast because of the tragedies that occurred on them, arousing the hearts and opening up the paths of teshuvah and reminding us of our evil actions and of the deeds of our fathers, which were akin to our current actions today, causing these tragedies to befall both them and ourselves. For by remembering these matters we will return to proper conduct, as the pasuk states (Vayikra 26:40), "And they shall confess their sin and the sin of their fathers."*[5]

---

2   *Yoel* 2:13.
3   *Yechezkel* 18:32.
4   *Yerushalmi, Yoma* 5a.
5   5:1.

These words pierce the heart! We are commanded to afflict ourselves on the four fast days that relate to the *churban*—not only to remember and to mourn, but primarily "to arouse our hearts and to open the paths of *teshuvah*."

In earlier times, before the *Kinnos* for Tishah B'Av were composed and popularized, it was customary to recite four *pesukim* from *Yirmiyahu*, as stated in *Maseches Sofrim*: "On Tishah B'Av—the four *pesukim* from *Yirmiyahu*, 'Have You utterly despised...' until 'For You have performed all of this...,'" and the two chapters, 'God, gentiles have entered Your portion...,' and 'By the rivers of Babylon...'"[6]

We see that they had the custom to recite two chapters of *Tehillim*, both of which discuss the *churban*, "Gentiles have entered Your portion" and "By the rivers of Babylon." But why were only four verses selected from the entire *Sefer Yirmiyahu*?

Let us analyze the content of these *pesukim*.

In chapter 14, the Navi states:

- *Pasuk* 19: "Have You utterly despised Yehudah? Have You loathed Tzion? Why have You smitten us, and we have no cure? [We] yearn for peace, but there is no goodness, for a time of healing, but there is trembling."
- *Pasuk* 20: "We know, Hashem, our wickedness, [and] the sin of our fathers, for we have [all] sinned against You."
- *Pasuk* 21: "Do not disgrace [us] for the sake of Your name; do not sully Your Throne of Glory; remember, do not revoke Your covenant with us."
- *Pasuk* 22: "Among the vanities of the gentiles, are there rain-givers? And if the heavens shall give of their drops, it is You Hashem our God and we shall hope to You, for You have performed all of this."

There are four fundamentals expressed in these *pesukim*:

1. A lament and cry over the depth of the pain and destruction, and over the rift between Yisrael and their Father in Heaven,

---

6   18:4.

about which the Navi weeps bitterly, "Have You utterly despised Yehudah? Have You loathed Tzion? Why have You smitten us, and we have no cure?"

2. Clear recognition that it has all come from Hashem, and we are not being smitten by chance: "It is You Hashem our God…for You have performed all of this."
3. Repentance and regret: "We know, Hashem, our evil, the sin of our fathers, for we have sinned to You."
4. A prayer and supplication that Hashem should have mercy on His name and on the remnant of His nation: "Do not disgrace [us] for the sake of Your name…remember, do not revoke Your covenant with us."

This is the essence of the duty of the day. The tears we shed at this bitter and mournful time do not just relate to the past—they are not about what once was and is no longer—they are tears of repentance and prayer, as we cry out and beg, "Do not sully Your Throne of Glory, remember, do not revoke Your covenant with us…for You have performed all of this."

TWENTY-FOUR

And He Is Bound in Chains

> *The message that came to Yirmiyahu from Hashem, after Nevuzeradan the chief executioner sent him from the Ramah, when he took him — and he was bound in chains — [from] among the entire exile of Yerushalayim and Yehudah who were exiled to Babylon.*
>
> Yirmiyahu 40:1

When we mourn over Tzion and Yerushalayim, the Beis Hamikdash and the Sanctuary, we ought to mourn not only the physical city of Yerushalayim, but also the Yerushalayim On High; not only the exile of the Jewish People, but also the exile of the Shechinah. We find this concept stated in *Megillah*, namely, that Hashem is also in exile together with the Jewish People.[1]

Thus, Chazal explain the aforementioned statement of Yirmiyahu, "And He was bound in chains," to be in reference to Hashem.

Similarly, Yechezkel HaNavi stated, "And I (*ani*) was among the exile."[2]

---

1 29a.
2 *Yechezkel* 1:1.

In other words, two prophets of Hashem relate the same message; not only are we in exile, Hashem is with us there too. In this light, *Tosafos*[3] give a profound interpretation of the prayer we recite during *Hoshanos*, "*Ani VaHo Hoshia Na.*" They explain that the two Divine names—**Ani VaHo**—refer to the two aforementioned *pesukim*, "**Va'Ani** *b'soch ha'golah*—And I was amongst the exile," and "**V'Hu** *assur ba'azikim*—And He was bound in chains," from which we learn that Hashem is with us in exile. Thus, the meaning of our supplication *Hoshana* is that **He should save Himself.**

In the *kinnah* composed by the *Alshich* to be recited during *Tikkun Chatzos*, it states: "Where has your Beloved gone, ascend with Him to the Heavens…I have sinned and **He is bound in chains**…Regarding this they eulogized and wept, they saw and lay in sackcloth…In the streets and marketplaces."

I have sinned, and He is bound in chains. Because of us and due to our sins, He is enchained. This is also the meaning of the following statement of Chazal: "**Woe to My children, for due to their sins I destroyed My Beis Hamikdash, burned My Sanctuary,** and exiled them among the nations."[4]

They state further: "Why are ashes placed upon the *aron kodesh* [during the public prayers on a fast day]…as if to say, 'I share their pain.'"[5]

Let us further consider the words of the Gemara in *Taanis*:

> *Rav Nachman said to Rav Yitzchak: "What is the meaning of the verse, 'In your midst is holiness, I shall not enter the city'? Because there is holiness in your midst, He shall not enter the city?" He replied: "This is how Rav Yochanan explained it: Hashem says, 'I shall not enter Yerushalayim in Heaven until I enter the Yerushalayim on Earth.'" But is there a Yerushalayim in Heaven? Yes, at it is stated, "The rebuilt Yerushalayim [shall be] like the city which is parallel to it."*[6]

---

3   *Sukkah* 45a.
4   *Berachos* 3a.
5   *Taanis* 16a.
6   5a.

The Heavenly Yerushalayim sits in mourning, waiting for the King of the world to enter it and for His Shechinah to reside there. Yet, He has vowed not to enter the Heavenly Yerushalayim until the earthly Yerushalayim is rebuilt.

There is a well-known comment of the *Vilna Gaon* that the statement, "I destroyed My Beis Hamikdash," refers to the Heavenly Beis Hamikdash, which sits uninhabited, for Hashem has sworn that He will not enter it. The words, "And I have burned My Sanctuary," refer to the Beis Hamikdash on Earth, which was destroyed by flames.

Thus, the pious and worthy men of previous generations mourned not over their bitter situation, the suffering and persecution, but over the pain of the Shechinah. That is why the *Perushim* declared after the *churban*, "How can we eat meat now that the *korbanos* have been discontinued? How can we drink wine now that the libations have been discontinued?"[7] They were not mourning their pain and distress, nor the blood of their sons and daughters that was spilled like water. Rather, they were mourning the discontinuing of the sacrifices and libations—"For these we cry." This is the essence of our supplication, "Restore Your Shechinah to Tzion Your city, and the order of service to Yerushalayim."

---

7   *Bava Basra* 60b.

TWENTY-FIVE

This I Shall Take to Heart

> *This I shall take to heart; therefore, I have hope.*
> Eichah 3:21

Megillas Eichah was written by Yirmiyahu HaNavi at the time of the destruction of the First Beis Hamikdash. In the third chapter, the prophet bemoans his fate—that he was Divinely ordained to accompany the people during this terrible time. Thus, the chapter opens, "I am the man, who has seen affliction, from the staff of His wrath."

If we examine this chapter, we notice something that calls for explanation. Up until *pasuk* 21, the Navi laments the *churban* and the exile, to the point that all hope seems to have been lost and not even the faintest ray of light penetrates the dark clouds. "Even when I cry out and scream, He has blocked my prayer."

Yet, in *pasuk* 21, the black clouds seem to part. The light of dawn shines through and a surge of hope fills the heart. "This shall I take to heart, therefore I have hope—Hashem is good to those who yearn for Him, to the soul that seeks Him—They are renewed in the morning, how great is Your faithfulness," and other such *pesukim* of faith and optimism.

This demands explanation. How do the light and darkness go together? How does the prophet emerge from despair to hope?

The answer may be derived from the following statement of Chazal: "'This shall I take to heart'—'this' only refers to Torah. And thus did David say, 'Were it not that Your Torah was my delight, I would have been lost in my suffering.'"[1]

Our holy Torah is what gives us hope during the most difficult times. It is what fortifies us with strength and courage in times of Divine concealment, times of destruction and desolation. It has stood for us from then until now; for in every generation there are those that arise against us to destroy us, and in the merit of the Torah, Hashem saves us from their hands.

During the *churban*, as the Beis Hamikdash was being destroyed and the Sanctuary went up in flames, Rabban Yochanan ben Zakkai asked of Vespasian Caesar, "Give me Yavneh and its scholars." Due to the *churban*, the kingship was to be discontinued from Yisrael, the princehood would be lost, the *Kehunah Gedolah* would function no longer, the service of the Kohanim and Leviim would cease, and the city of Yerushalayim—the joy of the land—would sit in mourning and sorrow. Yet Rabban Yochanan ben Zakkai saw with *ruach hakodesh* that despite all this, as long as "Yavneh and its scholars" would dwell proudly in Yisrael, they would sustain the nation and lead them with the might of their Torah and holy wisdom. They are the faithful guarantors that the Jewish People will endure in exile.

Yavneh and its scholars became the "Beis Hamikdash" of the exile. Chazal state in this regard, "'And I shall be for them as a miniature Sanctuary in every place they come'—these refer to the synagogues and houses of study in Babylon."[2]

"Yavneh and its scholars" became the place of residence of the Shechinah. After the *churban*, the Shechinah took its wanderer's staff and went into exile—from the Beis Hamikdash to Yavneh, and from there to the synagogues and houses of study, for our only remnant is the Torah. That is the meaning of the words of Chazal, "From the day

---

1   *Eichah Rabbasi.*
2   *Megillah* 29a.

that the Beis Hamikdash was destroyed, all that Hashem has in His world is the four *amos* of halachah."[3]

Throughout the exile, our only support and comfort is in Torah and its study. When our suffering compounds, when pain, sorrow, and fear overwhelm us and threaten to overcome us, we have always fled to the *beis midrash*, the miniature Sanctuary, and have found refuge and rejuvenation in the holy Torah.

Let us examine the words of the holy *Zohar* regarding the episode of Rabbi Eliezer and Rabbi Akiva.

In *Maseches Sanhedrin* the Gemara states:

> *When Rabbi Eliezer took ill, Rabbi Akiva and his colleagues came to visit him…he asked them, "Why have you come?" They replied, "We have come to learn Torah." He asked, "Why didn't you come until now?" They replied, "We didn't have the opportunity." He told them, "I would be surprised if they died a natural death." Rabbi Akiva asked him, "What will be with my death?" He replied, "Yours will be worse than theirs."*[4]

We wonder how Rabbi Akiva reacted to this frightening prophecy about his death and that of his holy colleagues—the Gemara does not elaborate.

However, that which the *Talmud* omits, the *Zohar* explains:

> *The Rabbis taught, when Rabbi Eliezer fell ill it was Erev Shabbos…the Sages of the generation went to visit him. He cursed them for not having served him, for we have been taught that serving [a Torah Sage] is greater than learning [from him]. "Akiva, Akiva, why didn't you serve me?" He replied, "Rebbi, I didn't have the opportunity." He grew angry, and said, "I would be surprised if you die a natural death." He cursed him that his death should be worse than the others. Rabbi Akiva cried and said, "Rebbi, **teach me Torah**."*[5]

---

3 *Berachos* 8a.
4 68a.
5 *Vayeira* 98b.

"Teach me Torah," Rabbi Akiva entreated. "*Rebbi*, teach me Torah" was the cry of his soul and the yearning of his heart. For it is our life and the lengthening of our days; only through words of Torah are we consoled and fortified against the waves of time, and the severity of the Attribute of Justice.

This I shall take to heart; therefore, I have hope.

TWENTY-SIX

I Await Him Every Day That He Should Arrive

> *I believe with complete faith, in the coming of Mashiach, and even though he may be delayed, nonetheless I await him every day that he should arrive.*
>
> The Thirteen Principles of Faith, Principle 12

These words are based on the *Rambam*.[1] We see that a person does not fulfill his duty merely by believing that Mashiach will come; he is obligated to yearn for him every day.

The *Rambam* similarly states in *Hilchos Mamrim*, "Anyone who doesn't believe in him **or does not await his arrival**, is not only a heretic with regard to the other prophets, but also with regard to the Torah and Moshe Rabbeinu."[2]

The *Rambam's* ruling may be based on the Gemara in *Shabbos*: "Rava said: When a person is brought to judgment, they ask him: Were you

---

1   *Peirush HaMishnah, Sanhedrin* 11.
2   11:1.

faithful in business? Did you set aside time for Torah study?...Did you await the salvation?"[3]

We see from here that a person is expected to await the salvation of Hashem, not just to believe in it.

There is a well-known comment of the Brisker Rav on the words, "And although he may be delayed, nonetheless I await him." In none of the other fundamentals of faith is there a question and answer—the first principle does not state that "although we see the righteous suffer and the wicked prosper, I nonetheless believe…" The fact that this clause is added here implies that aside from the belief in the coming of Mashiach, we are commanded to yearn for him and await his arrival.

Each person must examine himself and search in the depths of his soul to determine whether he truly awaits the arrival of the redeemer, or if it is just something to which he pays lip service.

Indeed, the great *tzaddikim* would sit and await the arrival of the redemption for their entire lives. My teacher, the Klausenberger Rebbe, *zt"l*, related about the *Yismach Moshe* that throughout his life, he would sleep with his stick and bag next to his bed, ready to go out and great Mashiach without delay.

My *rebbi* also related that on one occasion, this great *tzaddik* was expecting a visit from one of the great *tzaddikim* of the generation. When the distinguished visitor arrived, the *Yismach Moshe*'s attendant came to inform him, and opened the door to his study, saying, "He has arrived!" When the *tzaddik* heard this, he jumped up from his seat and announced with tremendous joy, "*Baruch Hashem* that we have merited the End of Days, and we are now going to greet Mashiach!" His yearning to greet the redeemer was immense, he felt it more strongly than the anticipation to receive a visitor due to arrive any moment.

We also merited to see my teacher, the Klausenberger Rebbe, *zt"l*, behave in this manner. All his life he yearned for the salvation with an intense and real yearning, as though each day he was sure that Mashiach would surely come. He fulfilled the words "I shall await him every day that he should arrive" in their fullest sense.

---

[3] 31a.

TWENTY-SEVEN

To Open the Paths of Teshuvah

The *Rambam* teaches us a novel concept regarding the four fast days that pertain to the *churban*:

> There are days on which all of Yisrael fast because of the tragedies that occurred on them, to arouse the hearts and to open up the paths of teshuvah, and to remind us of our evil actions and of the deeds of our fathers, which were akin to our current actions today, causing these tragedies to befall both them and ourselves. For by remembering these matters we will return to proper conduct, as the pasuk states (Vayikra 26:40), "And they shall confess their sin and the sin of their fathers."[1]

How does the *Rambam* know that the theme of these four fast days is that of *teshuvah*? Surely, they were instituted due to mourning for the *churban* of Yerushalayim and the Beis Hamikdash. In *Minchas Asher*,[2] I have explained that there are four principles pertaining to the fast days: repentance, mourning, appeasement, and commemoration, and the essence of these four fast days is that of mourning and distress.

---

1   *Hilchos Taanis* 5:1.
2   *Mo'adim* 2:36.

However, in truth, the source of the *Rambam* is very clear, for Chazal state, "Any generation in which it is not rebuilt, is considered to have destroyed it."³

(The point being contrasted is that it is not "as if it was destroyed," but as if that generation destroyed it.)

And if indeed we destroyed the Beis Hamikdash, it is our duty to do all we can to rebuild it. A person who breaks a vessel or destroys a house is liable to fix or rebuild it, or else reimburse the owner and pay for what he damaged. Were we to pay the damages for the *churban* it would be a terrible price of exile, death, destruction, harsh decrees, persecution, and cruelty, as took place during the first and second *churban*. Therefore, it is our responsibility to fix that which we damaged, and to rebuild the House that we destroyed.

The only means we have to rebuild what was destroyed and fix what was broken is through complete repentance.

Thus, Chazal state:

> They asked Rabbi Eliezer, "Were the later generations superior to the earlier ones?" He replied, "Their witness is the Beis Hamikdash. Our fathers removed the ceiling, as it stated, 'And he exposed the covering of Yehudah.' However, we tore down the walls, as it states, 'Uproot, uproot, until its very foundations.' This teaches us that any generation in which [the Beis Hamikdash] is not rebuilt, the Torah considers if they had destroyed it. What is the reason—for they did not do teshuvah."⁴

---

3   *Yerushalmi, Yoma* 5a.
4   *Yalkut Shimoni, Tehillim* 886; *Midrash Tehillim*, end of chap. 137.

TWENTY-EIGHT

With Fire You Are Destined to Rebuild It

It is known to us throughout the words of Chazal that the Heavenly Yerushalayim stands opposite the Yerushalayim on Earth. A Beis Hamikdash of fire is being rebuilt in the Heavens and, according to *Rashi*[1] and *Tosafos*,[2] it will descend from the Heavens, speedily in our days.

In this vein, the *Chasam Sofer*[3] explains the *pasuk* in *Tehillim*, "Hashem is the builder of Yerushalayim, He shall gather in the exiles of Yisrael."[4] The *pasuk*'s intent is that when the Jewish People gather in exile to mourn over Yerushalayim, Hashem is building the Yerushalayim On High.

It also seems clear that the vessels of the Sanctuary are similarly created from the mitzvos of Yisrael, by their holy service in areas related to these vessels. With their toil and diligence in Torah they help fashion the *Aron Ha'eidus*, and with the radiance and joy of Torah study they create the *Menorah*. Through their service of *tefillah* with proper intent they form the *Mizbei'ach*, and by means of their acts of kindness and

---

1 *Rosh Hashanah* 30a; *Sukkah* 41a.
2 *Shevuos* 15b.
3 *D'rashos* 2, 7 Av 5599.
4 147:2.

charity they fashion the *Shulchan*. The *B'nei Yissaschar* likewise states that every Jew must build his designated portion in the Heavenly Beis Hamikdash.⁵

The author of the *Levushei Serad* makes the following statement in his *sefer Arvei Nachal*:

> The future Beis Hamikdash, [may it come] speedily in our days, will descend from the Heavens built of fire, from the spirituality of Torah and good deeds that the Jewish People have performed since the Beis Hamikdash was destroyed. Just as with a physical building that is made of stones, one stone is placed upon the other until it is complete, and there are places where small stones are sufficient, such as in the middle of the wall, and other places require large stones, such as the cornerstones of the building and its foundations; the same is true with the spiritual building of fire. The mitzvos of those of lower stature are considered small stones, and the mitzvos of elevated tzaddikim are like large stones. The building is completed from all of them, and all of Yisrael have a portion in it—someone who does not have a portion in it shall not see it.⁶

My teacher, the Klausenberger Rebbe, zt"l, related that the holy *Divrei Chaim* once sat at his table wrapped in thought and declared, "I see in the Heavens that the entire Beis Hamikdash is ready and complete, and all that is lacking is the *Paroches*." One of the great *chassidim*, the tzaddik Rav Yehoshua of Tomashov, shouted with a heartfelt groan, "Let the Rebbe make the *Paroches*, and we will merit to see Mashiach." The *Divrei Chaim* thundered, "Indeed, we have already made the *Paroches*, but a wicked man has come from the lands of the West and torn it up."

We see that there is a great battle ensuing in Heaven in which one side is building and the other destroying. The righteous, with their mitzvos and good deeds, are building the Beis Hamikdash and perfecting its vessels; but at the same time, the wicked are destroying it.

---

5   *Maamarei Av* 3.
6   *Nitzavim, d'rush* 8.

Since the vision of the *Divrei Chaim*, approximately 150 years have elapsed, and we do not know what is lacking in the Heavenly Beis Hamikdash. Yet, one thing was revealed by two of the great Chassidic Masters, the *Admorim* of Ropshitz[7] and Kamernov.[8] They related that the holy Rebbe Elimelech of Lizhensk was once shown the *Mizbei'ach* that he built in the Heavenly Beis Hamikdash. When he asked, "Where is the *Aron*?" they replied, "When the *Aron* will be revealed, our righteous Mashiach will arrive, but the time is not yet ripe."

These are the words of the *Heichal Berachah*:

> For we have been taught by our Rabbis that every Jew chooses and builds a portion of the Beis Hamikdash. Our Master Rabbeinu Elimelech of Lizhensk had an elevation of soul, and they showed him that he had built the Mizbei'ach in the Heavenly Beis Hamikdash with his holiness. He asked them about the Aron and the Holy of Holies, to which they replied, "When [Hashem] desires that this be revealed, our righteous Mashiach will arrive, and it will be in the merit of the study of Torah for its own sake, with holiness and unification."[9]

Three points may be derived from his words: (1) Each individual has the responsibility to build his portion in the Beis Hamikdash, as stated above. (2) When the *Aron* is built, Mashiach will arrive. (3) The *Aron* will be built through the study of Torah with intent and holiness.

If so, the words of the great Chassidic Masters concur beautifully with the comment of the *Ohr Hachaim Hakadosh* at the beginning of *Parashas Tetzaveh*:

> By way of allusion, the pasuk can be explained by the statement of the sefer Zohar Chadash (Bereishis 8), that the Jewish People are redeemed from each of the four exiles in the merit of one individual. The redemption from the first exile was

---

7   Zera Kodesh, Parashas Ki Setzei.
8   Heichal Berachah, Parashas Ki Savo.
9   Parashas Ki Savo, p. 174.

in the merit of Avraham Avinu, the second in the merit of Yitzchak Avinu, the third in the merit of Yaakov Avinu, and the fourth will be in the merit of Moshe. For this reason, the exile is prolonged, for as long as they are not engaged in Torah and mitzvos, Moshe does not want to redeem a nation that is neglectful of the Torah.

We thus see that at the End of Days, the redemption will come about through the study of Torah, for it is only thereby that we build the *Aron*, which contains the *Luchos* and *Sefer Torah*.

We are experiencing the period of the birth pangs of the Mashiach, and the End of Days. It is our duty to complete and build the *Aron* of the Covenant of Hashem, so that we merit the coming of the redeemer.

And it is clear that the *Aron* is only built through the study of Torah, as explained above.

TWENTY-NINE

On Account of Kamtza and Bar Kamtza

Excerpts from a shiur given on Tishah B'Av

Rabbi Yochanan said: What is the meaning of the verse, "Happy is the man who is constantly afraid, and he who hardens his heart will fall in ruin"? Yerushalayim was destroyed due to Kamtza and Bar Kamtza, Tur Malka was destroyed due to a rooster and a hen, and Beitar was destroyed due to the side of a carriage.

Gittin 55b

When we study this *sugya*, we can make an astounding insight into the approach of Chazal. Rather than focusing on the wickedness of the Babylonians and Romans who destroyed our Beis Hamikdash, burned our Sanctuary, and mocked and blasphemed Heaven, this *sugya* emphasizes the sins of our fathers and their shortcomings that brought about this terrible destruction.

The significance of this is that we were commanded to commemorate the exile and *churban* only so that we should repent and correct the wrongdoing of our fathers.

Thus, the *Rambam* states:

> There are days on which all of Yisrael fast because of the tragedies which occurred on them, to arouse the hearts and to open up the paths of teshuvah, and it will serve to remind us of our evil actions and of the deeds of our fathers, which were like our current actions, causing these tragedies to befall both them and ourselves, for by remembering these matters we will return to proper conduct, as the pasuk states (Vayikra 26:40), "And they shall confess their sin and the sin of their fathers."[1]

His words are piercing: "For by remembering these matters we will return to proper conduct."

Elsewhere,[2] I have explained the episode recounted in the Gemara:

> The Rabbis taught: Rabbi Yehoshua ben Chanania once went to the great metropolis of Rome. They informed him, "There is a child imprisoned, with beautiful eyes and fine appearance, whose hair is arranged into curls." He went and stood at the entrance to the prison and announced, "Who has given over Yaakov to be plundered, and Yisrael to looters?" The lad answered, "Surely this is Hashem toward whom we have sinned, and they did not desire to follow in His paths, and they did not listen to His Torah." He declared, "I am sure that he will become an authority of halachah in Yisrael. I am not leaving until I redeem him with whatever sum they demand." It is said, he did not leave until he redeemed him with a large sum of money, and it was not long until he became an authority of halachah in Yisrael, and who was he? Rabbi Yishmael ben Elisha.[3]

The question arises: what did Rabbi Yehoshua ben Chanania see in the words of the young boy that made him sure that he would become a halachic authority for the Jewish People?

---

1   *Hilchos Taanis* 5:1.
2   Chapter 14 above.
3   *Gittin* 58a.

I explained this based on an inference that can be made from the *pasuk* quoted, which seems to contain an inherent contradiction. The *pasuk* starts, "Surely this is Hashem toward whom **we** have sinned"—indicating that it is we who have sinned and not others. But it then states, "**They** did not desire to follow in His paths to walk upon, and **they** did not listen to His Torah"—it was others who did not desire to follow in Hashem's paths or listen to His voice.

This *pasuk* teaches us that we must always consider our own deeds and shortcomings before finding others guilty and pinning the blame on them. How easy and how justifiable would it have been for this child to place the blame on many other parties. There was the Roman kingdom which, in its wickedness, destroyed the Beis Hamikdash and burned the Sanctuary; the *Biryonim*—the reckless ones, who incited the people to wage a war of bloodshed against the wishes of the Sages; and the *Tzedukim* and *Baytusim*, who aroused the Attribute of Justice with their iniquity.

And yet, before blaming all these parties who were indeed guilty, this young boy declared, "Surely this is Hashem toward whom **we have sinned**"—we are guilty ourselves.

In this manner, Chazal directed most of their comments in this *sugya* toward reflection on our own shortcomings, and the ensuing causes that brought about the *churban*. Let us analyze their words.

The Importance of Reflection

Rabbi Yochanan introduces our *sugya*:

> *Rabbi Yochanan said: What is the meaning of the verse, "Praiseworthy is the man who always fears, while he who hardens his heart will fall in ruin"?*
>
> *Rashi comments: "Afraid"—[someone who] worries to see the consequences of his actions, that nothing should go wrong if I do this.*

The *Maharsha* explains that after the people witnessed the destruction of Yerushalayim, they should have given thought, taken note, been worried, and mourned over Yerushalayim. Since they did not do so, they were punished, and their cities were also destroyed.

However, this explanation seems problematic, for it is stated, "Rabbi Yochanan said: What is the meaning of the verse, "Praiseworthy is the man who always fears, while he who hardens his heart will fall in evil"? Yerushalayim was destroyed due to Kamtza and Bar Kamtza, Tur Malka was destroyed due to a rooster and a hen, and Beitar was destroyed due to the side of a carriage."[4]

We see that Rabbi Yochanan also applied this *pasuk* to the destruction of Yerushalayim—not only to Tur Malka and Beitar. Further, these cities were destroyed due to their own sins, as the Gemara explains, not for a lack of mourning over Yerushalayim. Only Sechania of Egypt was destroyed because its residents did not mourn over Yerushalayim.[5]

Rather, it appears that Rabbi Yochanan meant to apply the lesson of this *pasuk* to Yerushalayim as well. Had they reflected over their actions and understood the consequences of their conduct, they would have corrected themselves and abandoned the evil of their paths, and the *churban* would have been avoided.

That is why Yeshayahu HaNavi lamented, "The ox knows its master, and the donkey the trough of its owner, but Yisrael does not know, **My nation does not give thought.**"[6]

Likewise, the *Rambam* enjoins us:

> Although the blowing of the shofar on Rosh Hashanah is a decree, there is an allusion to it: Arise O sleeping ones from your sleep, and slumbering ones awaken from your slumber, and examine your deeds and repent, and remember your Creator; those who forget the truth in the vanities of time, and all their lives pursue emptiness and vanity which will not help nor save. Look at your souls and examine your paths and actions, and let each man forsake his evil path and bad intent.[7]

---

4   Ibid. 55b.
5   Ibid. 57b.
6   *Yeshayahu* 1:3.
7   *Hilchos Teshuvah* 3:4.

This is what hinders us; that a person follows the desires of his heart, forgetting that for all of this, Hashem will bring him to judgment.

Kamtza and Bar Kamtza

> *Yerushalayim was destroyed due to Kamtza and Bar Kamtza.*[8]

Clearly, Yerushalayim was not destroyed due to the sin of one individual. It is stated explicitly in *Yoma*[9] and in the *Yerushalmi*[10] that the Second Beis Hamikdash was destroyed due to baseless hatred. However, this extreme case was brought as an example. It is also possible that this episode tipped the scales and caused the decree to be enacted.

At the same time this story has the added severity in that it tells of someone embarrassing another person in public. Further, Bar Kamtza pleaded for his life and offered to pay for the entire feast, yet the cruel host hardened his heart and ignored his plea, evicting him in shame and disgrace in front of all the guests.

Chazal state, "We have taught in a *Beraisa*, Rabbi Elazar said: Come and see how great is the effect of embarrassment, for Hashem assisted Bar Kamtza, and destroyed His Beis Hamikdash and burned His Sanctuary."[11] We find that they instituted several decrees in the aftermath of this episode, after seeing the power of embarrassment, and the severe Attribute of Justice that it arouses:

- The *Shaarei Teshuvah* states that as a result of this episode, it was instituted that the attendant should invite the participants to a feast from a written list.[12]
- The *Sefas Emes* states that as a result of this episode, Chazal instituted, "All that the host tells you, you must obey, **except for [if he tells you to] leave**," so that the host would not have the ability to disgrace a guest and evict him from the house.[13]

---

8   Gittin 55b.
9   9b.
10 Ibid. 4b.
11 Gittin 57a.
12 Orach Chaim 303:16, cited in *Mishnah Berurah*, sec. 47.
13 Pesachim 86b.

- The *Shulchan Aruch* states, "If a person loans his house for use as a synagogue, and then has a dispute with a member of the congregation, he may not forbid [the use of his house] unless he forbids it to the entire congregation together."[14] The *Mishnah Berurah* explains: "The reason appears to be that they were concerned about the disgrace of that individual, see *Gittin* 57. This would not apply if he would forbid it to everyone, for there is no embarrassment."[15]

There is an additional point in this story. Not only did the host sin by not caring for the honor of Bar Kamtza and evicting him in disgrace, but Bar Kamtza also sinned, slandering the Jews to the authorities and bringing great danger to the entire Jewish nation, ultimately causing the *churban*.

One sinned with an evil eye and the other sinned with evil speech, and between them, they destroyed the Beis Hamikdash. This is alluded to in the account given of how Bar Kamtza cast a blemish on the animal that the Roman Caesar sent as an offering to the Beis Hamikdash: "On the journey, he made a blemish on its lip; others say—on its eyelid."[16] **The lip** corresponds to the sin of *lashon hara* of Bar Kamtza, while **the eyelid** corresponds to the evil eye of the host.[17]

It is possible that Chazal are also inferring that even Kamtza held a degree of culpability for the *churban*, for it states, "Yerushalayim was destroyed due to **Kamtza** and Bar Kamtza." The *Maharsha* explains that the name Kamtza alludes to the characteristic of locusts, who hoard and gather for themselves, without giving thought to the needs of others. The *Ben Ish Chai* states in his *sefer Ben Yehoyada* that Bar Kamtza was actually the son of Kamtza, and the blame therefore extends to Kamtza, the father, for not seeing to it that his friend would also love his son. As such, he was concerned only about himself, not even about his close family.

---

14 *Orach Chaim* 153:16.
15 Sec. 88.
16 *Gittin* 56a.
17 See *Maharsha*.

The Debate between the Sages and Rabbi Zachariah ben Avkulas

> The Rabbis thought to sacrifice it because of peace with the authorities. Rabbi Zechariah ben Avkulas said to them, "People will say that blemished animals may be offered on the Mizbei'ach!" They thought to kill [Bar Kamtza], so that he would not go and inform on them. Rabbi Zechariah told them, "People will say that someone who makes a blemish on a sacrifice gets put to death!" Rabbi Yochanan said: The humility of Rabbi Zechariah ben Avkulas destroyed our Beis Hamikdash, burned our Sanctuary, and exiled us from our land.[18]

Let us analyze the dispute between the Rabbis and Rabbi Zechariah ben Avkulas.

The Rabbis foresaw the great danger and understood with their wisdom that this was a wicked plot to slander them before the Roman government, and therefore offered two solutions: (1) To offer the sacrifice despite it being blemished, for the danger to the life of an individual overrides the entire Torah, and how much more so the danger to the lives of the entire nation. (2) To kill the messenger, viewing him as an informer.

Yet Rabbi Zechariah ben Avkulas rejected both these suggestions, out of concern that "people will say..." This seems strange, for if he was not concerned about the Torah prohibitions of offering up a blemished animal or murder, why did he raise a lesser concern of "people will say"?[19]

It appears that there is more reason to be stringent about a concern that people will inadvertently derive a false halachah and a mistake will become rooted in the public than violating a Torah prohibition. This was the argument that Rabbi Zechariah presented to the Chachamim: Even if you are frightened of the Romans, and you therefore maintain that it is correct to offer up a blemished animal, we must nonetheless be concerned that people will draw a false conclusion—that a blemished

---

18 *Gittin* 56a.
19 This question is raised by the *Kovetz He'aros, Yevamos* 49; see his discussion of this topic.

animal may be offered on the *Mizbei'ach*. Even if you maintain that it is correct to kill the messenger, giving him the status of a *rodef*, we must worry that people will mistakenly think that someone who puts a blemish on a sacrifice is put to death. (See *Yam Shel Shlomo*,[20] who writes that a person must sacrifice his life rather than pervert or distort the Torah.)

However, it appears that the real basis for Rabbi Zechariah's position was that out of his goodness of eye and heart, he did not believe that there was a wicked plot to inform the Roman government. He assumed that this animal just happened to have become blemished, and the messenger was an innocent man with no intent of reporting to the government. His decision was therefore not to sacrifice the animal and not to kill the messenger.

That is the meaning of the statement of Rabbi Yochanan: "The **humility** of Rabbi Zechariah ben Avkulas destroyed our Beis Hamikdash, burned our Sanctuary, and exiled us from our land"—referring to his kind heart and benevolent eye.

The *Beis Yosef* cites the *Rashba* regarding the law of an informer: "Whoever acts with humility and has mercy on these people is being cruel to his generation, as it states (*Gittin* 56a): 'The humility of Rabbi Zechariah ben Avkulas destroyed our Beis Hamikdash.'"[21]

It is indeed obvious that if they had actually known there was a plot to slander them before the government, it would have been permissible to kill the messenger, as the *Meiri* states in *Bava Kama*:

> *It appears to me that if they see that someone is attempting to incite the authorities against the congregation, it is permissible to kill him. [This is derived] from the fifth chapter of Gittin, where it is stated, "I will go and slander them to the authorities...they thought to kill him so that he would not go and inform on them. Rabbi Zechariah told them...and they later*

---

20   *Bava Kama* 84, sec. 9.
21   *Choshen Mishpat* 388.

> said, 'the humility of Rabbi Zechariah ben Avkulas destroyed our Beis Hamikdash.'"²²

It would also have been permissible to offer a blemished sacrifice, as stated by the *Magen Avraham*.²³ He points out that we can derive from this episode that it is permissible to transgress a negative commandment out of fear of the authorities.

However, Rabbi Zechariah ben Avkulas was exceptional in his patience and excessive positivity of judgment, and did not suspect that this man was indeed wicked, as explained.

Learning the True Value of Money

> *Marta bas Baiysus was the wealthiest woman in Yerushalayim. She sent her attendant and told him, "Go and bring me semida [bread made from fine flour]." Meanwhile, it was sold out…She was barefoot, she said, "I will go and see if I can find something to eat." Some dung touched her foot, [and she was repulsed] and she died. Rabban Yochanan ben Zakkai applied to her the verse. "The soft and pampered among you, who did not tread her foot on the ground…" Others say, she ate a fig of Rabbi Tzadok, and was repulsed and died. For Rabbi Tzadok fasted for forty years so that Yerushalayim should not be destroyed. When he would eat something, it was visible from outside [his body]. When he was recovering, they would bring him dried figs, he would suck at them and discard them. When she was dying, **she took all her gold and silver and threw it in the marketplace, and said, "What do I need this for?!" In this regard, the pasuk states, "Their silver shall be cast in the streets."**²⁴*

It appears that there is an allusion here to the cause of the *churban*. The *Yerushalmi* states:

---

22   117b; *Shitah Mekubetzes* ibid.
23   656:8, cited by *Mishnah Berurah*, sec. 9.
24   *Gittin* 56a.

> However [at the time of] the second [churban], we know that they toiled in Torah, were careful in mitzvah observance and the separation of tithes, and possessed every good trait. But they loved money and had baseless hatred for one another. Baseless hatred is a grave matter, for it is equated to idolatry, adultery, and murder.[25]

If the root of their sin and wrongdoing was the love of money and pursuit of bribery, that must be what brought them to baseless hatred and jealousy, which destroyed our Beis Hamikdash and burned our Sanctuary.

This story comes to teach that all the silver and gold in the world is nothing but vanity. The wealthiest woman in Yerushalayim took all her silver and gold threw it into the marketplace, saying, "What do I need this for?!"

All the great wealth did not help or save her, and was likened to the dust of the earth.

If only we would learn from this and take this message to heart.

"'Mine is the silver and Mine is the gold,' says Hashem."[26] What gain does a person have from all his toil in this world? Only from his charity, loving acts of kindness, and good deeds.

"Give Me Yavneh and Its Scholars"

> [Vespasian Caesar] told him, "I shall leave and shall send someone else in my place. However, make a request of me and I will fulfill it." [Rabban Yochanan ben Zakkai] replied, "Give me Yavneh and its scholars, and the dynasty of Rabban Gamliel, and a doctor to heal Rabbi Tzadok." Rav Yosef applied to him the pasuk—some say it was Rabbi Akiva—"He diminishes [the wisdom] of Sages and makes their mind foolish," for he should have requested, "Leave [the Jewish People] be this time." However, he was concerned that [Vespasian Caesar] would not

---

25 Yoma 4b.
26 Chagai 2:8.

agree to so much, and even a partial salvation would not be achieved.[27]

This was the profound wisdom of the leader of the generation, Rabban Yochanan ben Zakkai—to save Yavneh and its scholars from the valley of death, so as to assure a remnant and continuity for the Jewish People.

As long as the Beis Hamikdash stood in its splendor, and the Jewish People dwelled securely—each man under his fig tree and vine; their eyes were raised to the Sanctuary where the Kohanim performed their service, while the Nasi of Yisrael stood at their head. At this time, the two pillars of authority leading the people were the *kehunah* and the princehood—the tribe of Levi and the tribe of Yehudah—and the eyes of the Jewish nation were raised toward them. The spiritual leadership was conducted by the Kohanim, who would offer the sacrifices, while the management of the nation was overseen by the Nasi, who stood in place of the kings of Yisrael who ruled in days of old.

However, once the Beis Hamikdash was destroyed and Yisrael were exiled from their land, both the *kehunah* and the princehood lost their elevated standing in the leadership of the people. Rabban Yochanan ben Zakkai understood, with his Divine inspiration and deep wisdom, that the scepter of authority must now transfer to the *beis midrash* and the "vineyard of Yavneh." The houses of study and yeshivos would be the only guarantee of the continuity of the people, and the great Sages would be the ones to lead the people throughout the duration of the exile. This was his request: "Give me Yavneh and its scholars."

Guaranteeing Jewish Survival in Exile

Another dimension of the wisdom of Rabban Yochanan ben Zakkai's request, "Give me Yavneh and its scholars," can be understood in light of a profound idea that my father, *zt"l*, pointed out to me.

If we reflect a little, we will realize that the pillars and foundations of Judaism, as we know and experience on a daily basis, are largely of a Rabbinic nature.

---

27   *Gittin* 56b.

Before Chazal forbade the conduct of business on Shabbos together with the other Rabbinic prohibitions, the day of Shabbos was much like a weekday. The people refrained from building and demolishing, from plowing and planting—but the shops were open and the people engaged in commerce. It was permissible to move money and tools. They could carry burdens from the house or courtyard to a *mavoi* (cul-de-sac), and from a *mavoi* to a *karmelis* (Rabbinic semi-public domain).[28]

Before the *Anshei K'nesses Hagedolah* instituted the order of *tefillah*, including Kaddish and *Kedushah*, it would seem that people did not go to shul or daven with a minyan, for their *tefillos* did not contain any sections that require a minyan, and the three daily *tefillos* had not been instituted.

Although Chazal state that Avraham, Yitzchak, and Yaakov each instituted *Shacharis*, *Minchah*, and *Maariv* respectively,[29] it is apparent from the *Rambam* that the intention is that they prayed these *tefillos*, not that they actually instituted them.[30]

It would therefore seem that they did not go to shul on either Shabbos or weekdays; rather, each person prayed alone in his home at a time of his choosing. Shabbos was like a weekday on which they did business, moved *muktzeh* items, and rode on horses and donkeys.

The foundations of Judaism are surely the daily order of service, the three daily *tefillos*, and the refraining from work on Shabbos and Yom Tov, all of which are Rabbinic.

This phenomenon can be explained as follows. In days of old, when the Beis Hamikdash stood, the eyes of the Jewish People were raised toward the Mountain of Hashem. Three times a year they would go on a pilgrimage to celebrate and see the Kohanim performing the *avodah*, and they would learn from them Torah and *yiras Shamayim*. This experience would fill the hearts of the Jewish People with the love and fear of Hashem.

---

28 See responsa *Chasam Sofer* 5, *Hashmatos* 195. I have elaborated on this elsewhere.
29 *Berachos* 26b.
30 *Hilchos Melachim* 9:1.

However, once the Beis Hamikdash was destroyed, the roads to Yerushalayim were laid desolate. There were no longer Kohanim performing their service or Leviim singing *shirah*, the *maamados* were discontinued, and the song ceased. Prophecy departed from Yisrael—and "without [prophetic] vision, the people will falter."[31] No remnant was left; no support remained.

This was until the *Anshei K'nesses Hagedolah* arose, together with the great Tanna'im and Sages of the Mishnah, and cast a new template of Jewish life. In place of the Beis Hamikdash that had been destroyed, they established miniature *batei mikdash*—the synagogues and houses of study—in which the people would gather for prayer three times a day, every day.

Shabbos Kodesh, the Sanctuary in time, became adorned as a festival. It discarded its weekday vestments and became enrobed in a new visage—that of complete rest and sanctity. The shops were shuttered and the marketplace deserted; instead, each man of Yisrael would sit in his home, studying Torah with song and praise, with honor and pleasure. The Six Days of Creation became sanctified with the holiness of Shabbos and were suffused with its blessing.

Judaism arose from the dust of the destruction and from the ashes of the burning Beis Hamikdash. It stood tall with pride and strength, with the Torah Sages as the leaders of the congregation, in place of the Kohanim of the Beis Hamikdash and the princes of Yisrael.

This is what Rabban Yochanan ben Zakkai saw with the eyes of his spirit at the destruction of the Second Beis Hamikdash—Yavneh and its scholars would be the single guarantee of continuity throughout the duration of the exile.

The *Yaaros Devash* points out that during the seventy years of the Babylonian exile, the level of the Jewish nation catastrophically plummeted, to the extent that they were marrying non-Jewish women, neglecting Shabbos observance, and the name of Hashem was forgotten.[32] By contrast, we have been living in exile for thousands of years, yet we

---

31   *Mishlei* 29:18.
32   Sec. 1, *d'rush* 6.

hold on to our purity and cleave to the mitzvos of Hashem. Surely, they were much greater than us, for "if they were as angels, we are as people."[33]

He elaborates—in his style—with a beautiful and profound treatment of this topic. However, his main theme is in line with what we have explained.

Protectors of the People

> He said, "Give me Yavneh and its scholars, and the dynasty of Rabban Gamliel, and a doctor to heal Rabbi Tzadok."[34]

We have already explained the profundity of Rabban Yochanan ben Zakkai's wisdom in his request for Yavneh and its scholars to be spared.[35] It appears that he asked for the dynasty of Rabban Gamliel, hoping that "the salvation of Hashem is in the blink of an eye,"[36] and He shall break the might of the wicked, uplift the pride of Yisrael, and speedily fulfill for them, "Restore our judges as before,"[37] returning the kingship to the house of David.

However, it seems puzzling that he asked for a doctor for Rabbi Tzadok, while tens of thousands were dying from thirst and starvation: "The tongue of a suckling cleaves to its palate out of thirst."[38]

The explanation is that Rabban Yochanan ben Zakkai knew that while the Attribute of Justice holds sway, there are a select few—the remnant of the great people of the nation—who call in the name of Hashem, and in whose merit the world endures. They are the ones who sustain the Jewish People with the power of their prayer and protect them with their righteousness.

This was the case with Rabbi Tzadok who sat for forty years in fasting and prayer, as Chazal state, "For Rabbi Tzadok fasted for forty years

---

33 *Shabbos* 112b.
34 *Gittin* 56b.
35 See p. 173, "Give Me Yavneh and Its Scholars," above.
36 Ri ibn Shuwib, *d'rashah* for the last day of Pesach.
37 *Shemoneh Esreh*.
38 *Eichah* 4:4.

that Yerushalayim should not be destroyed."³⁹ And as long as he sat in fasting and prayer, he did indeed protect the city.

A similar statement is made regarding the great Tanna, Rabbi Elazar HaModai:

> *We have taught: Rabbi Yehudah ben Rabbi Ilai said: Baruch, our rebbi, was expounding on the words (Bereishis 27:22), "The voice is the voice of Yaakov but the hands are the hands of Eisav"—he cried about what the hands of Eisav did to [Yaakov] in Beitar. Rabbi Shimon bar Yochai taught: Akiva, our rebbi, expounded on the verse (Bamidbar 24:17), "A star shall shoot forth from Yaakov"—Kuziva [Bar Kochva] shall shoot forth from Yaakov. When he would see Bar Kuziva, Rabbi Akiva would say, "This is our king, the Mashiach." Rabbi Yochanan ben Torta told him, "Akiva, grass will grow on your tongue and the son of David will still not yet come." Rabbi Yochanan said: [The pasuk refers to] the sound of Adaryanus Caesar killing in Beitar eighty thousand myriads. Rabbi Yochanan said, "Eighty thousand pairs of horn-blowers surrounded Beitar, each one appointed over several armies. Inside was Ben Kuziva, and with him were two hundred thousand men who had bitten off a finger [as a test of resilience]." The Sages sent to him, "For how long will you cast blemishes in Yisrael?!" He replied, "How else is it possible to check them?" They replied, "Whoever is unable to uproot a cedar of the Levanon while riding his horse shall not be including in the register of your army." He had two hundred thousand like this and two hundred thousand like that. When he would go out to battle, he would say, "Hashem, do not assist [us] but do not destroy [us]"—"Surely, You, God, have forsaken us, and God does not go out with our army" (Tehillim 60:12). For three and a half years, Adaryanus laid siege to Beitar.* **And Rabbi Elazar HaModai would sit on sackcloth and ashes and pray every day saying, "Master of the World,**

---

39   Gittin 56a.

do not sit in judgment today, do not sit in judgment today." *Adaryanus wanted to retreat. A certain Cuthite told him, "Do not go, for I will see what to do, and I will hand over the city to you." He entered through the city's outlet pipe. He went and found Rabbi Elazar HaModai standing and praying. He made out as if he was whispering in his ear. The people of the city saw him and took him to Ben Kuziva. They told him, "We saw this old man talking to your uncle [Rabbi Elazar HaModai]." He asked him, "What did you say to him and what did he tell you?" He replied, "If I will tell you, the king will kill me, and if I will not tell you, you will kill me. It is better for the king to kill me and not you." He then said, "[Rabbi Elazar] told me: I want to hand over the city [to Adaryanus]." [Ben Kuziva] went to Rabbi Elazar HaModai and asked him, "What did this Cuthite say to you?" He replied, "Nothing." "And what did you tell him?" He replied, "Nothing."* **He gave him one kick and killed him. Immediately, a Heavenly voice emanated and said, "Alas, the inept shepherd who has forsaken the flock—a sword against his arm and his right eye! His arm shall surely dry out and his right eye shall surely dim"** *(Zechariah 11:17).* **You have killed Rabbi Elazar HaModai, the arm of Yisrael and their right eye; therefore, the arm of that man shall surely dry out, and his right eye shall surely dim.** *Immediately, Beitar was captured and Ben Kuziva was killed. They went bearing his head to Adaryanus. He asked them, "Who killed him?" That Cuthite answered, "I killed him." He said, "Show me his body." They showed him his body, and they found a snake encircling it [that had killed him]. He said, "If not for God who killed him, who would have been able to kill him?!" He applied the pasuk (Devarim 32:30), "If not for that their Rock has sold them, and Hashem has closed them off."*[40]

---

40   *Yerushalmi, Taanis* 24a.

The mighty warrior Ben Kuziva relied on his own power and strength, believing that it had caused him to achieve all his success. He had an awesome army of brave and mighty soldiers—two hundred thousand soldiers who had each bitten off their own finger, and two hundred thousand who could uproot a cedar of the Levanon. They stood at his side to wage war and conquer the enemy, until his heart grew haughty, and he uttered disparaging words toward Heaven, saying, "Do not assist but do not destroy."

He did not realize that all of his mighty soldiers were like a feeble reed and fleeting dust. The one protecting the city was none other than the holy Tanna Rabbi Elazar HaModai, with his prayer, "Master of the World, do not sit in judgment, today, do not sit in judgment today." On the very day that Rabbi Elazar HaModai was killed, Beitar was conquered, and all of Ben Kuziva's mighty warriors fell into the hands of the enemy, who killed without mercy.

Rabbi Tzadok on the one side, and Rabbi Elazar HaModai on the other, were the righteous men of the generation, servants of Hashem in Torah and *tefillah*. They were the ones who stood by the Jewish People at times of crisis—to help, to save, and protect in the merit of their righteousness, their Torah and prayer—and the eyes of the Jewish People were turned to them.

Building Seven Altars

> "For Your sake, we were killed the entire day, we were reckoned as sheep to the slaughter." Rav Yehudah said: This was a woman and her seven sons. They brought the first one before the Caesar, and told him, "Worship this idol." He replied, "It is written in the Torah, 'I am Hashem your God.'" They took him away and killed him. They brought the next one...they brought the last one, and told him, "Worship this idol." He replied, "It is written in the Torah, 'Hashem you have designated...and Hashem has designated you today.' We have sworn to Hashem not to exchange Him for other gods, and He has sworn to us that He will not exchange us for another nation." The Caesar

said, "I shall throw down my ring, and you bend down and pick it up, so that people should say that you accepted the authority of the king." He replied, "Shame on you, Caesar, shame on you Caesar. If for your own honor, you are so concerned, for the honor of Hashem, how much more so." They took him to be killed. His mother said, "Give him to me so I can kiss him." She told him, "My son, go and tell Avraham your father: You performed an Akeidah on one altar, but I performed an Akeidah on seven altars." She also went up to the roof and fell and died. A Heavenly voice emanated and said, "The mother of sons is joyous."[41]

The tragic words of this woman seem very problematic. Was she boasting that she was greater than Avraham Avinu and sending him a brazen message?

Now, it is true that a person is not held accountable at a time of their distress,[42] and who can judge this heartbroken woman at the loss of her seven sons. However, if her words were inappropriate, Chazal would not have recorded them for all generations. If so, being that these were indeed appropriate and important words, we must understand what their true intent was.

I have explained elsewhere that when Avraham Avinu was tested with the ten trials and withstood them all,[43] he implanted the character strength within the Jewish People to withstand these tests that befall them for all generations.[44]

The *Ramban* teaches us that the actions of the Avos were a "**creative force**" for their descendants.[45] Their actions served not only as a symbolic pre-enactment of what would befall their descendants, but as a formative creation. The holy Avos, with their great and mighty deeds,

---

41 *Gittin* 57b.
42 *Bava Basra* 16b.
43 *Avos* 5:3.
44 *Sichos Minchas Asher on the Torah*, introduction to *Sefer Bereishis*.
45 Introduction to *Shemos*.

influenced all generations that followed and bestowed them with incredible fortitude and strength of character.

Chazal state similarly that Hashem told Avraham Avinu, "'Arise and walk in the land, its length and breadth, for I have given it to you'—so that it should be easy for your descendants to capture."[46]

The *Baal Haturim* comments on the *pasuk*, "And you shall love Hashem your God,"[47] that the word "ואהבת—and you shall love" is the same letters as "האבות—the forefathers." The deeper meaning within his comment is that we are commanded in this verse, "And you shall love Hashem your God…with all your soul—even if He takes away your soul."[48] Where do we draw this quality of self-sacrifice from? It is only from our holy forefathers, who offered their lives in sanctification of Hashem's name.

This righteous woman gave over her seven children in sanctification of Hashem's name. When her youngest son ascended to the Heavens in a storm, she proclaimed, "Go and tell Avraham your father: You performed an *Akeidah* on one altar, and with your great might, you gave your strength of character to me to perform an *Akeidah* on seven altars!"[49]

The Wickedness That Sealed the Decree

> Rav Yehudah said in the name of Rav, what is the meaning of the verse, "They robbed a man [together with] his home; and a person [together with] his lot"? It happened with a man who laid his eyes on the wife of his master, and he was an apprenticed carpenter. On one occasion [the master] needed a loan and he told him, "Send your wife to me and I shall lend her the money." She delayed with him for three days. He went and

---

46 *Bava Basra* 100a.
47 *Devarim* 6:5.
48 *Berachos* 54a; 61b.
49 However, the wording of the *Midrash Eichah* 1:21 does not accord with this explanation: "His mother came and hugged him and kissed him and embraced him, and whispered in his ear and told him, 'My son, my son, the youngest of them all, go and tell your father Avraham: Do not let yourself be proud; you performed an *Akeidah* on one altar, but I performed an *Akeidah* on seven altars.'"

> came to him, and asked, "My wife, whom I sent to you, where is she?" He replied, "I dismissed her right away, but I heard that the young lads jested with her on the way." He asked him, "What should I do?" He replied, "If you will listen to my advice, divorce her." He said, "Her kesubah is large." He replied, "I will lend you the money and give her the kesubah." He went and divorced her, and [the apprentice] went and married her. When the time came, he did not have the money to pay. He said, "Come and work for me to repay your debt." They were sitting and eating and drinking, and he was standing and serving them, and tears were streaming forth from his eyes and falling into their cups, and at that moment, the decree was sealed.[50]

This terrible story should disturb us profoundly and shock us to our very core. However, it remains to be analyzed: which *aveirah* did this wicked man actually transgress, and for which sin was their decree sealed?[51]

It appears, that there are times where the severity of an action is not limited to the level of a particular transgression, namely, whether it carries the punishments of *kareis*, death by the hand of Heaven, stoning or burning or similar. Rather, it is also dependent on the depravity of the wickedness, the perversion of character, and the depth of the iniquity and sin!

This wicked man, even if he did not violate one of the cardinal sins of the Torah—his sin was too great to bear. There was no limit to the evil of his heart, and the cry of the oppressed arose to the Heavens until **"the decree was sealed."**

---

50   58a.
51   While it does seem that he did, in fact, transgress serious violations: "Do not covet your neighbor's wife"—where not only did he desire her in his heart, he acted to bring about her divorce from her husband and married her instead. This transgression is one of the Ten Commandments. He transgressed, "Distance yourself from falsehood," in that he lied to him in a manner that caused him harm and pain. He secluded himself with his neighbor's wife and transgressed the Torah prohibition of *yichud*. Nevertheless, even these aveiros do not seem to be that severe so as to incur destruction.

I have elaborated elsewhere that even regarding practical halachah, the "intent of the Torah" is also taken into consideration, not just the positive and negative mitzvos.[52]

We have been commanded to cleave to the mitzvos of Hashem: "Emulate Him—just as He is gracious and compassionate, so should you be gracious and compassionate."[53] Where was the compassion of this cruel man? Where was his graciousness—to rebel against the person who did kindness to him, to steal his wife from him, and all his money together with her, and to disgrace him to the very dust, and to further degrade him to see his beloved wife living with his apprentice—is there an extreme wickedness worse than this? "They were sitting and eating and drinking, and he was standing and serving them, and tears were streaming forth from his eyes and falling into their cups."[54]

---

52 *Minchas Asher, Devarim* 51.
53 *Shabbos* 133b.
54 See the glosses of the *Yaavetz* to that *sugya*.

THIRTY

He Proclaimed for Me a Mo'ed

Tishah B'Av that falls on Shabbos

> The fast of the fourth [month] and the fast of the fifth [month], the fast of the seventh [month] and the fast of the tenth [month] will become [times of] gladness and joy and days of festivity for the Jewish People, and truth and peace shall you love.
>
> Zechariah 8:19

A question arises with regard to Tishah B'Av that coincides with Shabbos. In the future, when Tishah B'Av becomes a time of gladness and joy, will we celebrate it on Shabbos, or on Sunday (the day to which the fast is currently postponed)?

The *Chasam Sofer* asserts that the Yom Tov will take place on Sunday. He proves this from the fact that we omit *Tachanun* on Tishah B'Av that is delayed until Sunday.[1] The *pasuk* states regarding Tishah B'Av, "He proclaimed for me a *mo'ed*." The term *"mo'ed"* is usually used to refer to

---

1   *Toras Moshe, Devarim*, s.v. "Me'reish."

a festival, thus the *pasuk* implies that Tishah B'Av is something of a festival; hence, we omit *Tachanun*. Given that *Tachanun* is even omitted on the postponed fast day, we must conclude that the aspect of *mo'ed* is similarly postponed to the next day.

However, it may be argued that the characteristic of *mo'ed* is really dependent on the fast; they are interlinked—like two sides of the same coin. When the fast is postponed to Sunday, that day is considered a *mo'ed*. However, in the future, when the day will emerge from sorrow to joy, it would seem that the Yom Tov could occur on Shabbos, like any other festival that falls on Shabbos, which is not postponed.

It should also be noted that even today, when Tishah B'Av occurs on Shabbos, we do not recite the prayer of "*Tzidkasecha*," as it is called a *mo'ed*.[2] We see that the Shabbos is also considered a *mo'ed*. If we accept the approach of the *Chasam Sofer* we must conclude that both days are considered a *mo'ed*, not just Sunday.

However, there is a more fundamental question on the premise of the *Chasam Sofer*: What is the connection between the verse, "He proclaimed for me a *mo'ed*," and the assurance of the prophet that the days will become *Yamim Tovim*? After all, out of the four fast days, only Tishah B'Av is called a *mo'ed*, but they will all become times of gladness and days of festivity in the future.

In truth, however, there is room to suggest that in the future, when we merit that Hashem returns to His people, **both** of these days will indeed become a period of gladness and joy each year and not only when Tishah B'Av falls on Shabbos, for a very simple reason.

The Gemara states, "Rabbi Yochanan said: Had I been in that generation, I would have established [the fast day] on the tenth, for the majority of the Sanctuary was burned on that day. However, the Rabbis maintain that the onset of the tragedy is more significant."[3]

We see that there is reason to fast on the tenth of Av, as the majority of the *Heichal* was burned on that day. This is the view of Rabbi Yochanan, but the Rabbis ruled that the onset of the tragedy is more significant.

---

2   *Shulchan Aruch, Orach Chaim* 552:12.
3   *Taanis* 29a.

Elsewhere, I have explained that both opinions are true, and on the occasions when Tishah B'Av is postponed, we fast on Sunday not only because we cannot fast on Shabbos, but also because that was the day on which the majority of the *Heichal* burned.

Chazal did not want to establish two days of fasting because of the danger to health, as well as to avoid excessive mourning, and therefore argued over whether to fast on the ninth or the tenth. The *Yerushalmi* states that there were great Amora'im who indeed fasted on both the ninth and the tenth because the majority of the *Heichal* burned on that day.[4] This was the practice of Rabbi Yehoshua ben Levi, Rabbi Avin, and Rabbi Levi. The *Tur* states that it is only because of the difficulty involved that we do not fast for two days,[5] and even on Yom Kippur, where there is *s'feika d'yoma* (doubt as to the correct date[6]), we do not fast for two days. In the future, however, when the days will be times of gladness and festivity, all opinions agree that it will be appropriate to give thanks and praise, and to celebrate *Yamim Tovim* both on the ninth—when the suffering started, as well as the tenth—when the majority of the *Heichal* burned.

Rashi likewise states, "'Gladden us like the days of our affliction'—gladden us during the days of our Mashiach like the number of days of our affliction in exile, and the number of years in which we saw suffering."[7]

May the Beis Hamikdash be rebuilt speedily, and we merit that these days become *Yamim Tovim*—times of gladness and eternal joy—speedily in our days.

---

4   *Taanis* 25b.
5   *Orach Chaim* 558.
6   See *Beis Yosef* there.
7   *Tehillim* 90:15.

THIRTY-ONE

Rebbi Sought to Abolish Tishah B'Av

Tishah B'Av that falls on Shabbos

> *Rabbi Elazar said in the name of Rabbi Chanina: Rebbi [Rabbi Yehudah HaNasi]…sought to abolish Tishah B'Av, but they did not agree with him. Rabbi Aba Bar Zavda said before him: That was not what happened; rather, it was Tishah B'Av that coincided with Shabbos, and it was postponed until after Shabbos. Rebbi maintained that once it has been postponed, it should be deferred completely, but the Rabbis did not agree.*
>
> Megillah 5b

According to the Gemara's conclusion, Rebbi sought to abolish a Tishah B'Av that coincides with Shabbos, for once it has already been postponed, it should be canceled—but the Rabbis did not accept his opinion.

Rebbi Sought to Abolish Tishah B'Av   189

The *sefer Avodas Yisrael* of the Maggid of Kozhnitz, cites the Chozeh of Lublin who states that Rebbi sought to abolish Tishah B'Av completely by hastening the arrival of Mashiach and the complete redemption.[1] However, the Rabbis did not agree with him, for we may not force the arrival of the redemption.

He explains that when Tishah B'Av occurs on Shabbos, the sanctity of Shabbos, with its pleasure and joy, overrides the mourning of Tishah B'Av. In reality, there are two aspects to Tishah B'Av. While we must feel the pain of the *churban*, we must correspondingly strengthen our recognition of the kindness of Hashem and His abundant mercy toward us, even in the midst of the destruction and exile. We must strengthen our faith that the salvation of Hashem comes in the blink of an eye, and that the Beis Hamikdash will speedily be rebuilt.

The Gemara in *Makkos* relates that Rabbi Akiva and his colleagues ascended to Yerushalayim and saw a fox emerging from the Holy of Holies.[2] They began to weep, but Rabbi Akiva laughed. These two feelings of sadness and joy were merged together, one corresponding to the other. Clearly, Rabbi Akiva also mourned over the *churban*, and his great colleagues also had feelings of joy about the redemption—they differed only with regard to which should be the focus.

All agree that even in the depths of the pain of exile, we should endeavor to see the hand of Hashem in His abundant mercy. Chazal state:

> It is stated (Tehillim 79), "A song of Asaf, God, gentiles have entered Your heritage." The pasuk should surely have written: "A weeping of Asaf; a wailing of Asaf; a lament of Asaf!" But it is comparable to a king who made a wedding house for his son, and plastered, decorated, and adorned it, but his son went astray. Immediately, the king went to the wedding house, tore down the curtains, and broke the reeds. The son's teacher took a reed flute and started playing music. They asked him, "The king has upturned the wedding house of his son and you are

---

1   *Parashas Mas'ei.*
2   24b.

playing music?" He replied, "I am singing because he upturned the wedding house of his son but did not vent his wrath upon his son." Likewise, they said to Asaf, "Hashem has destroyed His Sanctuary and Beis Hamikdash and you are singing?" He replied, "I am singing for He vented His wrath on wood and stones and did not vent His wrath upon Yisrael, as it is written, 'And He lit a fire in Tzion that consumed its foundations.'"[3]

In the merit of our faith and joy, even in the depths of the sorrow of exile, we will hasten the redemption. This is the meaning behind Rebbi's attempt to abolish Tishah B'Av that coincides with Shabbos. When Tishah B'Av coincides with Shabbos and we rejoice and delight with faith, yearning for the day that will be entirely Shabbos and rest for eternity—this has the power to uproot Tishah B'Av, and hasten the footsteps of Mashiach, speedily in our days.

---

3   *Eichah Rabbah* 4:14; see *Tosafos, Kiddushin* 31b, s.v. "*Istayah.*"

THIRTY-TWO

Comfort, Comfort My People

> *"Comfort, comfort My people," says your God.*
> Yeshayahu 40:1

Chazal state that just as the Jewish People were smitten with a double measure of punishment (as it states, "For she has been smitten by the Hand of Hashem doubly for all her sins"[1]), so they will be comforted with a double measure of consolation (as it states, "Comfort, comfort My people, says your God").[2]

This seems puzzling. Surely, the *pesukim* tell us, "The Rock whose actions are perfect, for all His ways are justice,"[3] and "Yours, Hashem is kindness, for You repay each man **according to his deeds**."[4] Why should they be punished in a **double measure**? Does the law of double compensation (as stated regarding a thief caught with stolen goods) apply to all transgressions in the Torah?

---

1 *Yeshayahu* 40:2.
2 *Yalkut Yirmiyahu* 312.
3 *Devarim* 32:4.
4 *Tehillim* 62:13.

Furthermore, what is the meaning of a double consolation?

The explanation appears to be as follows. The Jewish People were smitten in their exile with the pain and suffering that they endured at the hands of their persecutors, but also with the deep Divine concealment they experienced when they were challenged, "Where is your God?" Indeed, *Rashi* tells us that at the very moment that Yosef was being sold as a slave, a miracle was performed for him, for Arabs typically carried naphtha (which is foul-smelling), but the caravan carrying him was bearing fragrant spices.[5] The *chachmei ha'mussar* explain that the purpose of this miracle was to show him a sign—that Hashem bestows His mercy even during times of pain and suffering, for "I share their pain."

Throughout their exile, however, the Jewish People have passed through desolate and death-ridden lands and have slept in the valley of tears, and they have not always seen the sign from Heaven attesting to Hashem's kindness. In this manner, they were doubly smitten. (There is an allusion to this in the fact that the *pasuk* depicts the Divine concealment with a double expression, "*V'Anochi* **haster astir** *panai ba'eis ha'hi*—And I shall surely conceal My Face at that time."[6])

Thus, in the future we shall be doubly consoled. Hashem will end our suffering and we will merit to see "the day that is entirely good," and we will be further comforted when we realize that all the troubles that befell us were actually good; in reality, Hashem did not withhold His kindness and goodness from us for even one moment.

In this light, we can explain the Gemara in *Pesachim*:

> "On that day, Hashem shall be One and His name shall be One." Is He not already One now? Rav Acha bar Chanina said: This world is not like the World to Come. In this world, upon hearing good tidings, we recite, "Blessed is the Good and Beneficent One," and upon hearing bad tidings, we recite, "Blessed is the

---

5   *Bereishis* 37:25.
6   *Devarim* 32:18.

True Judge." However, in the World to Come, it will be entirely "The Good and Beneficent One."[7]

Many wise men have grappled with this statement, for it implies that the only difference between this world and the next is in the text of the berachah we recite, not in their actual respective experiences. It does not state that this world contains both good and bad, but the World to Come will be entirely good; rather, what will change in the World to Come will be the way in which we relate to our experiences, and the blessing we thus recite.

It appears to be, that in the World to Come, we will recite the berachah of *Ha'tov V'Hameitiv*—The Good and Beneficent One" over those calamities upon which we already recited the blessing of "*Dayan Ha'emes*—the True Judge" in this world. For at that time, our mouths will be filled with laughter and our tongues with song over the "bad tidings" that befell us in this world. When Hashem will remove the dust from our eyes, and we realize that all our difficult experiences were actually great kindnesses to us from Hashem Yisbarach, we will then recite the blessing of *Ha'tov V'Hameitiv* over all that happened to us.[8]

It Is I, Only I, Who Comforts You

In this vein, it appears that we can explain why the word "*Anochi*" is repeated in the *pasuk*, "*Anochi, Anochi Hu menachemchem*—It is I, I, Who comforts you."[9]

When Yaakov Avinu was concerned about descending to Egypt, Hashem appeared to him and said, "*Al tira mei'reda mitzrayemah...***Anochi** *eired imecha mitzrayemah,* **v'Anochi** *a'alcha gam alo*—Do not be afraid to descend to Egypt; **I** shall descend to Egypt with you, and **I** shall surely bring you back up."[10]

---

7 50a.
8 I have since seen that the *Tzelach* cites this explanation in the name of the great *maggid*, Rabbi Ephraim MiReisha.
9 *Yeshayahu* 51:12.
10 *Bereishis* 46:3–4.

In light of the above, it would seem that the first promise that "I will descend to Egypt with you" was not an assurance of the redemption, but an assurance that Hashem would be with him in his suffering, that Hashem shares our pain and exile, and that the Attribute of Justice is really the Attribute of Mercy. The second promise, however, was the promise of the redemption.

Thus, the verse, "Anochi, Anochi Hu menachemchem—It is I, only I, Who comforts you," refers to the promise of "**Anochi** eired imecha mitzrayemah—I will descend to Egypt with you," and that of "**V'Anochi** a'alcha gam alo—And I shall surely bring you back up." These two assurances correspond to the two aspects of consolation stated in the *pasuk*, "Comfort, comfort My people, says your God."

THIRTY-THREE

Hashem Is the Builder of Yerushalayim

> *Hashem is the Builder of Yerushalayim,*
> *He shall gather in the dispersed ones of Israel.*
>
> Tehillim 147:2

The *Chasam Sofer* explains this *pasuk* as saying that when the dispersed Jews are gathered, Hashem builds the Yerushalayim in Heaven.[1] In other words, when Yisrael gather in their places of exile to mourn over Yerushalayim and lament its destruction, it causes the Heavenly Yerushalayim to be rebuilt.

A source for this can be found in the *Kuzari*:

> When people are aroused and inspired to feel love for this holy place, great returns are achieved in the progress toward the desired objective, as it states, "You shall arise and have mercy on Tzion; for it is the time to favor it, for the time has come. For Your servants have desired its stones, and have favored its dust." This means that Yerushalayim shall be rebuilt when the

---

1   Vol. 3, *d'rashah* for seventh of Av 5599.

> Jewish People will yearn for it with an intense longing, until they find favor in its very stones and dust.[2]

We see that Hashem shall arise and have mercy on Tzion, when Yisrael shall favor its dust and desire its stones, out of love of the holy site.

This is the meaning of the statement of Chazal, "Whoever mourns over Yerushalayim shall merit to see its rejoicing; and whoever does not mourn over Yerushalayim shall not merit to see its rejoicing."[3]

The *Meiri* comments, "Whoever acts out of rote on this day, and does not arouse his heart to mourn over Yerushalayim, will not see its rejoicing. It need not be said that a person must not forget about the mourning entirely."[4]

We see that it is not sufficient to go through the motions of mourning; a person must arouse his heart to mourn over Yerushalayim and the *churban*. Anyone who does so will merit to see the joy of Yerushalayim, but "whoever does not mourn over Yerushalayim will not merit to see its joy." Similarly, it is taught in a *Beraisa*, "Whoever eats meat and drinks wine on Tishah B'Av, in his regard the verse states, 'And their sin was on their bones.'"

Commenting on this statement of the Gemara, the *Ritva* writes the following astounding words:

> This means that his bones will not be resurrected at techiyas ha'meisim in the future, to be present at the Third Beis Hamikdash [which is the lot of] those who die in exile who yearned for salvation, regarding whom the pasuk states (Daniel 12), "Fortunate is the one who yearns and arrives at those years." However, it is possible that such a person will still be resurrected for the day of judgment that follows the time of Mashiach.[5]

---

2   5:27.
3   *Taanis* 30b.
4   Ibid.
5   Ibid.

His words are somewhat enigmatic, but they are explained in the responsa of the *Radvaz*:

> My dear friend, you asked me regarding the time of resurrection about which you received a tradition from your ancestors—that it will be close to the seventh thousand-year period, together with the onset of "the Shabbos of the world," which will be entirely a period of rest. However, you are troubled; for if this is so, the righteous and pious people who died while sanctifying Hashem's name in exile shall not see the goodness of the Jewish People and shall not rejoice in their happiness!
>
> *Answer:* My entire life, I was bothered by this question—until I saw the words of the Ritva, citing his teachers, that there shall be two resurrections: One [resurrection shall be] exclusively for the righteous people who died in exile, which shall be close to the coming of Mashiach, and they shall merit [to experience] all the days of Mashiach with both body and spirit, and shall see the good of Yisrael and the building of the Beis Hamikdash, and shall rejoice with happiness in return for their service…Aside from this, there shall be another general resurrection, which shall be close to the onset of Shabbos, as I have received in a tradition. This is called "the world of techiyah," regarding which it states, "And many of those asleep in the dust shall awaken…"[6]

We see that the *Radvaz* transmits and elaborates upon the tradition mentioned by the *Ritva* that there will be two separate periods of *techiyas ha'meisim*. Those who suffered the yoke of exile, who mourned for Yerushalayim and yearned for salvation—they will arise first and will witness the good that befalls the Jewish People with the rebuilding of Yerushalayim and the splendor and joy. However, those who did not mourn over Yerushalayim will arise only with "the onset of Shabbos," for the World to Come.

---

6   Sec. 3, 644 [1069].

A similar concept is expressed by the *Shibbolei Haleket*:

> *The Rabbis taught: Whoever eats and drinks on Tishah B'Av shall not see the joy of Yerushalayim, and whoever mourns over it will merit to see its joy, as it states, "Be glad with Yerushalayim and exult with it, all its lovers; delight with it joyfully—all those who mourn over it." Someone who mourns over it shall see its joy. My brother Rabbi Binyamin, zt"l, explained that someone who mourns over it is worthy of seeing its consolation—even if it would be at the end of time, and he is listed among the group of tzaddikim who are inscribed for life in Yerushalayim and are worthy of the redemption. Whoever does not mourn over it is not worthy of seeing its consolation, and even if he lives at the time of the redemption, he is reckoned among the group of wicked who do not believe and are not worthy of the redemption, as we find regarding Egypt—that all those who did not believe in the redemption died in the three days of darkness. We and all Yisrael who believe in the salvation of our God will merit "to see the pleasantness of Hashem and to visit His Sanctuary" and to be comforted with the consolation of Tzion, with all of Yisrael, Amen. "Like a man whose mother comforts him, so shall I comfort you, and in Yerushalayim you shall be comforted."*[7]

At the end of his responsum, the *Radvaz* states:

> *Always remember this matter, for it is a source of great consolation for those enduring the suffering of exile and the yoke of subjugation, that their eyes will yet see Tzion as a tranquil abode and the Sanctuary in its perfection, and the holy avodah established in its proper order, speedily in our days, Amen.*

May our portion be among the mourners of Yerushalayim, and may we thus merit to witness it rejoicing, speedily in our days.

---

7 Motzaei Tishah B'Av, *Seder Taanis* 274.

Netzach Yisrael
The Eternity of Israel

THIRTY-FOUR

An Address at Auschwitz

Adar 5769

We stand here at these moments on ground that is soaked with Jewish blood. In this accursed spot, sixty-five years ago, rivers of blood mingled together with rivers of tears. The blood of the elderly mixed with the blood of *gedolei Yisrael* and that of small children who never tasted sin. Roughly one-and-a-half million *kedoshim* met their deaths here and rose heavenward in flames and smoke, not even meriting a Jewish grave.

An oppressor of the Jews, the likes of whose evil and iniquity has not arisen since the inception of the Jewish People, tried on this spot to carry out his "Final Solution" for the Jewish Problem: to eradicate us and our memory, to destroy and annihilate every Jew, young and old, with cruelty that knew no limits and which had no parallel in all of human history. No one was spared and no clemency was given. All were led through together like sheep to the slaughter, family after family, holy communities with their leaders and teachers. All walked to their deaths with the words "*Shema Yisrael, Hashem Elokeinu, Hashem Echad!*" on their lips.

Smoke and fire hid the face of the sun, darkness descended on the world, and we saw the fulfillment of the prediction: "And I will surely conceal My face on that day."[1] Mankind lacks the words to express, and the wisdom to grasp, the *middas ha'din* that was deeper than the grave.

---

1   *Devarim* 31:18.

Should a person begin to contemplate and endeavor to understand this decree, he hears a voice from on high, warning, "Turn back—this is a decree that I have issued!"

When B'nei Yisrael sinned with the Golden Calf and were punished with a plague, Moshe Rabbeinu, our faithful shepherd, pleaded: "Make Your ways known to me."[2] Chazal explain that Moshe was asking for the reason why the righteous often suffer while the wicked enjoy prosperity.[3]

My feeling with regard to this Gemara is that Moshe was asking specifically about the fate of Klal Yisrael. His request was touching on a question which penetrates to the deepest depths. We know that "Beloved are the people of Israel, for they are described as children of the Omnipresent; it is indicative of an even greater love that it was made known to them that they are described as children of the Omnipresent—as it is said: 'You are children to Hashem your God.'"[4] Hashem chose us above every other nation. Why, then, do we suffer more than any other nation in the world? Why are we visited with death and destruction while other nations lead lives of peace and tranquility?

The Jewish People had just received the Torah from Sinai—thereby becoming Hashem's people—and they had already sinned and been punished, as our Sages have taught:

> Ulla said: How shameful is the bride who is unfaithful while still in her bridal chamber. Rav Mari, the son of Shmuel's daughter, said: What is the pasuk that reflects Ulla's sentiment? "While the King was still at His banquet, my perfume [gave out its fragrance], etc." (Shir Hashirim 1:12).[5]

The Jewish nation had just stood at the foot of Har Sinai and declared, "*Naaseh v'nishma*—We will do and we will hear," and then, immediately thereafter, sinned and were punished with a plague. It was about this that Moshe asked concerning "*tzaddik v'ra lo, rasha v'tov lo.*"

---

2 *Shemos* 33:13.
3 *Berachos* 7a.
4 *Avos* 3:14.
5 *Shabbos* 88b and *Gittin* 36b.

Hashem answered him:

> He said, "You will not be able to see My face, for no human can see My face and live." Hashem said, "Behold! There is a place near Me; you may stand on the rock. When My glory passes by, I shall place you in a cleft of the rock; I shall shield you with My hand until I have passed. Then I shall remove My hand and you will see My back, but My face may not be seen."[6]

I have often said that there are two aspects with regard to understanding Hashem's ways: seeing His face and seeing His back. This can be compared to a person who sits and listens to Torah from his *rebbi*. If he sees his *rebbi*'s face, his understanding is sound and complete. However, if he only sees the *rebbi* from behind, his understanding will be limited and incomplete. Thus, Rabbi Yehuda HaNassi said: "The reason that I am sharper than my colleagues is that I saw Rabbi Meir from behind. Had I seen him from the front, I would be even sharper."[7]

Rashi explains: "I saw Rabbi Meir from behind"—that is, when I learned Torah from him, I sat in the row behind him.

This is what Hashem was saying to Moshe: "You will see My back, but My face may not be seen." Even Moshe Rabbeinu, the father of all prophets, the faithful shepherd who spoke with Hashem directly, neither saw nor apprehended Him except from behind. "You will not be able to see My face, for no human can see My face and live."

When Hashem showed Moshe Rabbi Akiva's Torah, and then showed him Rabbi Akiva's death, Moshe cried out in anguish, "This is Torah, and this is its reward?" As Chazal relate:

> *Rabbi Yehudah said in the name of Rav: When Moshe ascended On High, he found Hashem as He was sitting and attaching crowns to some of the letters. Moshe said before Him, "Master of the Universe, who is holding You back [from giving the Torah as it is]?" Hashem said to him, "There is one man who*

---

6 *Shemos* 33:20–23.
7 *Eiruvin* 13b.

is destined to live at the end of many generations—Akiva ben Yosef is his name—and it is he who will expound upon each and every crown heaps and heaps of halachos."

Moshe said, "Master of the Universe, show him to me!"

Hashem said to him, "Turn around and see what is behind you."

Moshe found himself in Rabbi Akiva's class. He went and sat at the end of eight rows of students, but as he listened to the give-and-take between Rabbi Akiva and his students, he did not understand what they were saying, and Moshe became disheartened. However, once they reached a certain matter that required a source, Rabbi Akiva's students asked him, "Rebbi, from where do you know this?" Rabbi Akiva replied to them, "It is a halachah transmitted orally to Moshe at Sinai." Upon hearing this, Moshe's mind was relieved.

He returned and came before Hakadosh Baruch Hu and said before Him, "You have someone like this, and You gave the Torah through me?!"

Hashem said to him, "Quiet! Thus did the thought arise before Me [that is, this is part of My greater plan, to which you are not privy]."

Moshe said before Him, "Master of the Universe, You have shown me his Torah, now show me his reward."

Hashem said to him, "**Turn around** and see what is behind you." Moshe turned around and saw that people were weighing the flesh from [Rabbi Akiva's] body in the meat market in order to sell it. Moshe said before Him, "Master of the Universe! This is Torah and this is its reward?!"

Hashem said to him, "Be silent! Thus did the thought arise before Me."[8]

---

8   *Menachos* 29b.

What Hashem was saying to Moshe was, "I have stated: 'You will see My back, but you may not see My face!'"

There are decrees that are too exalted to be grasped by the human intellect. They are decrees issued from before Hashem, concerning which we "cannot see His face."

Such was the death of the great Tanna, Rabbi Akiva ben Yosef.

And so, too, was the Holocaust.

A Holocaust in which more than six million holy Jews were murdered. A Holocaust in which more than a million pure Jewish children were cruelly put to death. *Rebbis* and their *talmidim*, many great Torah luminaries and a thousand years of Jewish life went up in flames, leaving behind nothing but smoke and ashes.

We have no explanation. We don't know the reason. I know that many have tried to speculate, to explain why Hashem brought about this great punishment. They have tried to postulate as to the nature of the transgression that brought about the Holocaust, but this is a mistake. In response to such an enormous catastrophe, such terrible and irreparable pain that the eye cannot witness, the mouth cannot speak, and the ear cannot hear, we are forced to say, "גזירה היא מלפני—This is My decree!" To anyone who attempts to find an explanation, we tell him, "חזור לאחוריך—Turn back!"

We have survived the terrible exile not in the merit of our wisdom or with the answers which we produced to explain Hashem's ways. We have survived in the merit of our perfect *emunah*, our belief that everything that the Merciful One does is for the good. We have survived the difficult exile in the merit of our attachment to Hashem and His Torah and in the merit doing His mitzvos, not in the merit of philosophical treatises regarding reward and punishment.

There was a pious man in the Kovno ghetto by the name of Reb Moshe Goldkorn. The tale of this man's courage and self-sacrifice is recounted by the *gaon* Rabbi Ephraim Oshry. In his *sefer Sheilos U'Teshuvos Mima'amakim*,[9] he recounts the following story.

---

9   Vol. 5, sec. 6.

As Pesach 5702 (1942) approached, Reb Moshe was worried about how they would obtain *matzos* to fulfill the mitzvah of the festival. Since he had a special permit from the authorities allowing him to leave the ghetto from time to time, Reb Moshe bravely smuggled a bit of wheat flour into the ghetto, purchased from neighboring Lithuanian gentiles.

On *erev Pesach*, a Nazi soldier discovered Reb Moshe as he was preparing to bake the *matzos*, and he beat him mercilessly. Broken and shattered, with blood pouring from his mouth, Reb Moshe knocked on Rabbi Oshry's door. When Rabbi Oshry opened the door and saw Reb Moshe beaten and bleeding, he was shocked and shaken.

"I have a question for his honor, the Rav," Reb Moshe said.

I imagine that the Rav expected Reb Moshe to ask the most difficult of questions, about why bad things happen to righteous people and good things happen to the wicked. Perhaps he would ask, "This is Torah, and this is its reward?!"

But these were not the questions on Reb Moshe's mind. Instead, he asked, "I am from a *chassidishe* family and, as such, I have never eaten matzah that has been soaked in liquid. But that *rasha* broke all my teeth, so that I have no teeth left with which to chew. Am I now to abandon the custom of my fathers in order to fulfill this great mitzvah, or should I cling to my fathers' custom and not eat soaked matzah?"

It is not in the merit of our answers that we have come through the awful exile still clinging to Hashem, but rather the merit of our questions. Questions like the one Reb Moshe Goldkorn asked. It is in the merit of our profound recognition of, "Why do you concern yourself with these hidden things of the Merciful One? What you are commanded to do, you must do."[10]

We are privileged to have my father, the *gaon* and *chassid*, *shlita* [zt"l], standing here at my side. Approximately sixty-five years ago, he last stood on this spot and saw his parents and five of his brothers and sisters sent to the left, to their cruel deaths in the gas chamber, while he was sent to the right toward backbreaking labor, suffering and

---

10   *Berachos* 10a.

degradation. He has just recited Kaddish to the Master of the Universe, our Merciful Father, in the memory of his father and mother and the six million *kedoshim* who were sacrificed here. He and all the other survivors who have merited rebuilding the house of Israel with devotion and incredible strength—they stand witness to the fact that *Netzach Yisrael lo yeshaker*: the Jewish People will live forever.

That wicked enemy (may his name be blotted out) tried in this place to carry out his "Final Solution." He and his evil cohorts will be remembered in ignominy. Their guilt will never be assuaged, and disgrace will blacken their memories forever. But the people of Israel are alive and endure!

Avraham Avinu, father of the Jewish nation, declared: "וְאָנֹכִי עָפָר וָאֵפֶר—I am but dust and ash."[11] I believe that these words may be understood on a deeper level, in light of *Tosafos*'[12] explanation of the prayer, "And let my soul be like dust to all," that dust is the only thing in the world that cannot be destroyed. The *Maharshal* there adds:

> *I also heard: just as dust is something that everyone tramples on, yet it ultimately covers over all those who trampled on it, so, too, let me be thus to all those who torment me.*

When Avraham Avinu said, "I am but dust and ash," he was prophesying about his children and his children's children and his descendants to the end of time.

What is the meaning behind comparing his descendants to ash? Our Sages teach:

> *There is a certain bird named chol, concerning which it is written, "I will live as long as the chol" (Iyov 29:18).*
>
> *The students of the Academy of Rabbi Yannai say: This bird lives for one thousand years, and after one thousand years a fire issues from its nest and consumes it—leaving over an egg equaling its original size, from which it once more grows limbs and continues to live. Rabbi Yudan, the son of Rabbi Shimon,*

---

11 *Bereishis* 18:27.
12 *Berachos* 17a.

> says: It lives for one thousand years, and after one thousand years its body disintegrates and its wings fall off—but an egg the size of its original body remains, from which it once more grows limbs.[13]

Chazal have compared Klal Yisrael to the *chol* bird that lives for a thousand years. At the end of that time, a fire erupts from its nest and consumes the bird until nothing is left of it but ashes. And then, miraculously, it is reborn from the ashes to live another thousand years.[14] That wicked one, *yemach shemo*, predicted a Reich that would endure for a thousand years, and indeed he was right, for this is the secret of the Jews. The Nazi Reich, may its name and memory be blotted out, is gone. There is nothing left of it in the world. But Am Yisrael rose from the dust and ashes of the furnaces and was reborn to live another thousand years.

Thus did Avraham Avinu say: "I am dust and ashes."

This is the secret of our people's eternal existence. It is a miracle within a miracle. As Rabbi Yaakov Emden said: The existence of Klal Yisrael, like a lamb among seventy wolves, is a greater miracle than that was done for our forefathers in Egypt, on the Yam Suf and in Eretz Yisrael.[15]

This terrible place, where that wicked man, descendant of the wicked Eisav, tried to implement his "Final Solution," indeed symbolizes the final solution of an eternal people.

And this is the final solution: eternal redemption at the End of Days. "On that day, Hashem will be One and His Name will be One."

---

13 *Bereishis Rabbah*, *Parashah* 19, *siman* 5.
14 See *Sanhedrin* 100b and *Rashi* ibid., that the bird known as *chol* lives forever.
15 *Sulam Beis Kel* in the *Beis Yaakov* siddur.

THIRTY-FIVE

Parchment Burning, Letters Ascending

Chazal expound the word Bereishis to mean: "For the sake of the Torah, which is called reishis, and for the sake of Israel, who are called reishis." Therefore, they said that one who is standing near a dying person at the moment his soul departs is obligated to tear his clothes (Mo'ed Katan 25a). To what can this be compared? To seeing a Sefer Torah that is being burned. The kedushah of every Jew's soul is literally like the kedushah of a Sefer Torah.

Nefesh Hachaim, shaar 4, chapter 11

Hashem gave the Torah to Israel, and the soul of Israel is the body of the Torah, for Israel are the six hundred thousand letters of the Torah. It thus emerges that Israel is the Torah, for every person in Israel is a letter in the Torah.

Kedushas Levi, Bamidbar

> *We have seen in both early and later sources that the number of all the letters in the Torah is six hundred thousand. The name ישראל alludes to this, for it is an acronym for "יש ששים ריבוא אותיות לתורה—There are six hundred thousand letters in the Torah." Therefore, all of Israel numbered six hundred thousand, like the letters in the Torah, and the soul of every member of Israel has a particular mitzvah and an attachment to one letter. This is virtually universally agreed upon, and is mentioned in the Zohar and in the holy sefer Shnei Luchos Habris in numerous places.*
>
> P'nei Yehoshua, Kiddushin 30

We have here three of the great Torah sages of the generations, who illuminated our eyes with the idea that all the souls of B'nei Yisrael are linked to the letters of the Torah. Likewise, in the introduction to *Responsa Beis HaLevi*, the author writes that the body of Israel has the sanctity of the parchment of a *Sefer Torah*, and the souls of Israel are like its letters.

I have often thought that this is what lies behind the abundant joy we witness at every *hachanasas Sefer Torah*. Throngs of Jews sing and dance with all their might, with a joy that knows no limits. What is the source of this joy? After all, most shuls already have a *Sefer Torah* in their *aron kodesh*, and all members of the congregation have been reading from it regularly. Why, then, is there such overwhelming joy at a *hachnasas Sefer Torah*? It is because on those occasions, a longing arises from the recesses of our souls to connect to the letters in the *Sefer Torah*.

And indeed, we are witness to the fact that, down through the centuries, when wicked people among the nations of the world have plotted to destroy the Jewish People, they begin by pouring their out wrath on our *Sifrei Torah*. First they degrade and mock our *Sifrei Torah* without pity, and then they go out to war against the nation of Israel with the same ruthlessness. Apparently, they sense that the soul of our nation is inextricably tied to the holy Torah. *"Yisrael v'Oraisa"*: the Jew and the *Sefer Torah* came down from Heaven intertwined—and there are times when they also ascend to Heaven intertwined!

Indeed, on a visit to the Jewish community of Berlin some years ago, I was shown the central square in which *Sifrei Torah* were burned, even before Jewish blood was spilled.

The Gemara relates the following episode:

> *When Rabbi Yose ben Kisma became ill, Rabbi Chanina ben Tradyon went to visit him. [Rabbi Yose] said to [Rabbi Chanina]: "Chanina, my brother! Do you not know that this evil [Roman] nation has been granted dominion from Heaven: they have destroyed [Hashem's] House, burned His Sanctuary, killed His pious ones and caused His nobles to perish, and they still endure? Yet I have heard that you sit and engage in Torah and convene gatherings in public [to disseminate Torah], with a Torah scroll resting openly on your lap! [Why do you endanger yourself so?]"*
>
> *[Rabbi Chanina] said to [Rabbi Yose]: "From Heaven they will have mercy."*
>
> *[Rabbi Yose] responded to [Rabbi Chanina]: "I am saying something sensible to you—and you are telling me that from Heaven they will have mercy?! I would be amazed if they do not burn you and the Torah scroll in fire!"*
>
> *…It was said that it was just a few days later when Rabbi Yose ben Kisma died. All the great men of Rome went to bury him and they gave great eulogies for him. Upon their return, they encountered Rabbi Chanina ben Tradyon, who was sitting engaged in Torah study and convening gatherings in public [for its dissemination], with a Torah scroll resting on his lap [all in open violation of their edicts]. They brought him and wrapped him in a Torah scroll, encircled him with bundles of vine shoots and set them on fire. [The Romans] then brought tufts of wool,*

> soaked them in water and placed them over Rabbi Chanina's heart, so that his soul would not depart the body quickly.
>
> [Rabbi Chanina's] daughter said to him: "Father! Must I see you in such a state?"
>
> He answered her: "If I alone were being burned, it would be a difficult thing for me. However, now that I am being burned and the Torah scroll is with me, He who will seek retribution for this insult of the Torah scroll will seek retribution also for my insult."
>
> As the fire raged, [Rabbi Chanina's] disciples said to him, "Master, what do you see?"
>
> He answered them: "The blank parchment is burning and the letters are flying upward!"[1]

Tosafos explain the background to the disciples' question, "What do you see?":

> For it seemed appropriate to them that he should see something wondrous, or angels, or some other such thing. Alternatively, they heard the sound of the letters flying away and did not know what it was.

Chazal have stated that the words of Torah are "like a hammer that shatters a stone, sending shards in multiple directions,"[2] so that we, too, have been granted permission to explain and elucidate. It is possible that the disciples' question did not refer only to the seeing which takes place with the physical eye, but also to "seeing" with the eyes of the mind and heart. Those were days of wrath and fury, a time of death, harsh decrees, and destruction, when each day surpassed the one before in suffering. Now, the leader of the generation is rising heavenward in flames, and a despairing cry bursts from his disciples. "*Rebbi*, what do you see?"

---

1 *Avodah Zarah* 18a.
2 *Sanhedrin* 34a.

Is there hope for us in the end? Will there be a reward for everything we've done? We remain behind like a flock without its shepherd!

Rabbi Chanina answers: Do not let your spirits waver or your hearts melt with fear. There is hope for you in the future and a reward for your actions. "The parchment is burning"—the wicked regime may burn and destroy our bodies, which are compared to the parchment of a *Sefer Torah*, but the soul of our nation is not susceptible to destruction. "And the letters are taking flight"—the souls of B'nei Yisrael are linked to the letters of the Torah that are flying into the air. At the time when Hashem so desires, the letters will return to their places and many *kehillos* will once again congregate together, for Hashem has promised that the Torah will never be forgotten from His children.

It was specifically this conduct—which rose above nature and above the intellect with *mesirus nefesh*—that led to the Roman destruction and the salvation of Klal Yisrael, as *Tosafos* relate in the name of the work *Maaseh Hamerkavah*: "As a result of the episode with Rabbi Chanina ben Tradyon, a great destruction was decreed on Rome."[3]

Rabbi Chanina ben Tradyon saw "אותיות פורחות." This expression has two meanings:

- First, as the parchment burned, the letters took flight (פרחו).
- Second, when Hashem so desires, those same letters are destined in the future to return to their places and put down roots that will flourish and bloom (לפרוח)—as it says: "And you will see and your heart will exult, and your bones will flourish (תפרחנה) like grass" (*Yeshayahu* 66:14). The letters will one day bloom again and bear the fruit of the Tree of Life in the establishment of the eternal Torah, forever and ever!

---

3 *Avodah Zarah* 2b.

THIRTY-SIX

Remembering the Holocaust

I was asked for my opinion regarding saying *kinnos* in the memory of the victims of the Holocaust, and, if it is appropriate to do so, whether to say them on Tishah b'Av or at some other time.

In truth, this question is one that has caused me much distress and consternation, for it would seem that we should certainly shed tears day and night over this catastrophe that has befallen our people. In the *kinnos* of Tishah b'Av, we recite a *kinnah* about the destruction of three Jewish communities in Germany during the Crusades: the holy *kehillos* of Speyer, Worms, and Mainz, with their thousands massacred. That suffering was like a drop in the sea of blood and tears that befell our fathers during the Holocaust. On the other hand, we find no *kinnos* written about the victims of the Inquisition in Spain and Portugal, nor was a special fast day established to commemorate them, despite the fact that thousands were slaughtered *al kiddush Hashem*. We see that not every situation of suffering resulted in saying *kinnos*, such that it is difficult to know what the parameters of this matter are.

Moreover, in the *kinnah* that we recite on Tishah b'Av over the destruction of those *kehillos* in Ashkenaz ("*Mi yiten roshi mayim*"), we declare: "However, [we] cannot add a [new] day [of mourning] over ruin and conflagration." This indicates that we are not supposed to add a specific day to remember subsequent times of suffering and catastrophe, and we therefore recite this *kinnah* on Tishah b'Av. On the other hand, the *Sefer HaRokeach* writes: "In Worms, they fast over the calamity that took place on Rosh Chodesh Sivan. The custom there is to read the Rosh Chodesh Torah reading in the morning, and in the afternoon to read '*Vayechal*' and add the haftarah, '*Dirshu*.'"[1] We see that in Worms, they fasted on Rosh Chodesh Sivan in commemoration of the community's decimation, and it is clear that they are referring to the same episode—for the *kinnah* that we say on Tishah b'Av also cites the "third month," which is Sivan![2] How can this be reconciled with the idea that we do not introduce additional fast days for later calamities?

It would appear that the resolution is that in the place where the disaster took place, such as the Worms *kehillah* itself, there, they would fast and say *kinnos* on the anniversary of the event. In other places, however, they did not establish a special date for mourning but continued only to say *kinnos* on Tishah b'Av.

The matter, however, is not fully resolved. The *Magen Avraham*[3] states that one should fast on the twentieth of Sivan, when thousands of Jews were killed and whole communities were decimated in Poland during the "*Gezeiros Tach v'Tat*."[4] This fast day was widely accepted throughout the Jewish world, to the point where the *Taz*[5] wrote that, although the *Shulchan Aruch* states that when a public fast is decreed on a Monday or Thursday, we do not substitute the reading of "*Vayechal*" instead of the regular Torah reading, nevertheless, on the twentieth of Sivan we do, for it marks a terrible destruction, the likes of which had not occurred since the time of the *Churban* itself, and a fast was accepted among all of Klal Yisrael.

The *Pri Megadim* there, and the *Beis Yaakov Siddur*, in the introduction to the selichos for that day, state that even in their time, more than a century after the *Gezeiros Tach v'Tat*, they all continued the custom

---

1   *Siman* 212.
2   In the year 4856.
3   *Siman* 580, sec. 9.
4   The Chmielnicki Massacres of 1648–49.
5   *Siman* 566, sec. 3.

of reciting these selichos, and in particular the selichos written by the *Shach*, who personally experienced these events. (The *Tosafos Yom Tov*, who likewise suffered through these bloody rampages, wrote *kinnos* about them entitled "*Megillas Eivah*.")

From all of these sources, we see that a specific day was established for fasting and prayer and they did not attach it to Tishah b'Av, and the pillars of Torah learning upon whom all of Israel rely—the *Shach*, the *Taz*, the *Tosafos Yom Tov*, and the *Magen Avraham*—agreed to this custom without objection. So the matter requires further investigation.

In terms of practice, I am greatly perplexed regarding this matter. In the years after the Holocaust, we had many great and holy Torah leaders who had personally suffered terribly during the war. Among them were the Klausenberger Rebbe, *zt"l*, who lost his wife and eleven children, the holy Rebbes of Belz and Satmar, and the Imrei Emes, *zt"l*, who was rescued from Poland at the start of the war. In addition, we had the *Chazon Ish*, Rabbi Yizchak Zev Soloveitchik of Brisk, and many other Torah giants and leaders, yet they did not establish a fast or special *kinnos*. As is well known, the *Chazon Ish* was once asked for his opinion about the establishment of a "Yom HaShoah" to commemorate the Holocaust, and he answered, as the *kinnos* instruct, that an additional day is not supposed to be established to commemorate destruction. Are we better than they, to establish what these great men did not?

I know of some great leaders of our time who wrote *kinnos* to commemorate the Holocaust, each in his own style, and certainly it is acceptable to recite them on Tishah b'Av. However, I personally remain silent, as I prefer not to do what my fathers and teachers did not.

Nevertheless, even if we do not recite these *kinnos*, we are obligated to remember the destruction of our people every day. We were commanded to remember not only the destruction of the Beis Hamikdash through the four fast days that the prophets established, but also the days of suffering and tribulation throughout the ages, as we have mentioned above. How much more so with regard to the horrors of the Holocaust, the suffering of which is unparalleled in our history!

We are additionally called upon to remember the thousands of stories of *mesirus nefesh* for Torah and mitzvos of those who died to sanctify the Holy Name—may Hashem avenge their blood!

Written in tears and pain,
Asher Weiss

THIRTY-SEVEN

Educating Children about the Holocaust

To my dear friend, HaRav Sholom Friedman, *shlita*,

First, I would like to offer my blessing to his honor for his tremendous activity in instilling the memory of the Holocaust within the Chareidi educational system. I view this activity as one of utmost importance. We have been commanded to remember the glory of *yetzias Mitzrayim* and the giving of the Torah forever, as well as the times of destruction and exile on the four fast days that our prophets established.

Throughout the generations, our Sages likewise instituted special *kinnos* to commemorate the destruction of the communities of Ashkenaz and many other tribulations throughout our history. It is inconceivable that we would not commemorate our six million pure and holy brothers, who ascended to heaven in a storm of blood, fire, and smoke.

With regard to your question as to what should be emphasized when we teach our youngsters about the Holocaust and what educational lesson can be derived from this commemoration, there are three principles that we must emphasize when teaching about the Holocaust.

1. First, we must simply teach about the enormous catastrophe that happened to our people because of Hashem's wrath. We

should teach about the *kehillos* that were destroyed and the holy people who were murdered, and the multitudes from among Hashem's people who were lost, and we must mourn them. As for the cruel suffering of the war, this must be related with moderation, in a manner that is age-appropriate to the students, so as not to cause them excessive sadness or introduce into their young hearts questions and doubts regarding their faith. This must be done with care and sensitivity.

2. Second, they should be told about the many episodes of self-sacrifice for mitzvos and the incredible acts of *chessed* that were performed in the valley of death, not only by the *gedolei Yisrael* but also by many simple Jews. There were numerous cases where individuals gave up their meager ration of bread, hardly enough to keep them alive, in order to save someone else from dying of hunger. I heard such stories from my father, *zt"l*, who personally witnessed and experienced such things during those bitter years. I heard an incredible example of *mesirus nefesh* in the Holocaust from my master and teacher, the Klausenberger Rebbe, *zt"l*. With tremendous determination and self-sacrifice, he endured the entire period of suffering under the Nazi regime without partaking of any cooked food, for fear that it might be unkosher. He subsisted on crusts of bread and raw potatoes stolen from the accursed wicked oppressors.

3. Most importantly, however, you must emphasize the amazing revival that we merited in the wake of the Holocaust and in the period that followed. The rejuvenation of the Jewish People was an open miracle. I heard many times from my Rebbe, *zt"l*, from my father, *zt"l*, and my mother, may she be spared for long life, that when the survivors were rescued from the inferno and found themselves alive—one person out of an entire community or two members of an extended family—none of them believed that there was a future for Torah and for Yiddishkeit. And then—a miracle within a miracle—the body of Israel was resurrected, and those dry bones became the embodiment of the

prophecy: "You will see and your heart will exult, and your bones will flourish like grass."[1]

The Jewish People returned to its holy land to build and to be rebuilt. The holy *yeshivos* and Chassidic courts once again struck root, grew, and flourished, and Klal Yisrael shook off the dust of the ghettos and the ashes of the crematoria and took wing like eagles, to shine with sevenfold brightness.

It is one of the mysteries of the Almighty that it is specifically out of the most terrible destruction and the darkest darkness that the lights of salvation and redemption glow.

Tosafos say something astounding:

> We find in the work Maaseh Hamerkavah that as a result of the episode of Rabbi Chanina ben Tradyon, a great destruction was decreed on Rome.[2]

They are referring to that which is related about Rabbi Chanina ben Tradyon,[3] who taught Torah publicly in defiance of the Roman edict against that practice, with a *Sefer Torah* resting on his lap. When the Romans caught him, they wrapped him in a *Sefer Torah* and set them both on fire. The great Tanna was burned *al kiddush Hashem* while enveloped in the *Sefer Torah*.

When his students asked him, "What do you see?" Rabbi Chanina replied, "The parchment is burning and the letters are flying up." I have explained elsewhere (see above, chapter 33), that those brokenhearted students with shattered spirits meant to ask, "Our great Master, what do you see with the eyes of your elevated spirit? Is there hope for our future and a reward for our actions? Behold, the leader of the generation, in whose shadow we sought to live, is rising to heaven in a storm, while we remain behind like a flock with no shepherd and like a ship buffeted on stormy seas with no captain to guide it!"

---

1   *Yeshayahu* 66:14.
2   *Avodah Zarah* 2b, s.v. "Romi."
3   Ibid. 18a.

Their teacher answered, "The parchment is burning." The body of every Jew is compared to the parchment of a *Sefer Torah*, but the souls of Israel are bound to the letters of the Torah. They can burn our bodies, but the Jewish soul is eternal. There is no power in the world that can eradicate it: "The letters are flying up."

The students, and the entire nation, were broken and shattered, but through His *hashgachah*, Hashem saw fit to decree great destruction upon Rome specifically through this episode, as described in the *Maaseh Hamerkavah*, mentioned by *Tosafos*.

In other words, it was specifically at this terrible time, as the students witnessed such a horrific manifestation of *middas ha'din*—that *din* turned to *rachamim* and destruction was decreed for Rome.

I am neither a prophet nor the son of a prophet. Prophecy is gone and not even *ruach ha'kodesh* manifests itself in our times. We do not plumb the depths of the Divine mysteries and we do not know at what moment or through which particular incident destruction was decreed for the wicked regime of Hitler's Thousand-Year Reich, may his name be blotted out. However, by the time the war ended, Germany was in ruins, millions of Germans had been killed, and the Nazi movement had become an object of disgrace for all time.

Because of their cruel persecution of Hashem's people, that nation was sentenced to a great destruction.

So we have seen all through history: it is specifically in the wake of destruction and despair, when it seems to us that all hope is lost and there is no future for our people, miraculously and in defiance of all expectation we have merited a period of tremendous growth and flourishing.

After the destruction of the Second Beis Hamikdash, when Yerushalayim was devastated and the Jewish People had been massacred and plundered—that was when the great Tannaim appeared: Yavneh and its Sages, Rabbi Yochanan ben Zakkai's students and the students of those students, the Sages of the Mishnah, and after them the Amoraim and the Sages of the *Talmud Bavli* and *Yerushalmi*. It was the quintessential period of growth and splendor for the Oral Torah.

This is one of the secrets of Divine conduct in this world, that pride *follows* a fall and that specifically in a period of degradation characterized by murder, pillage, and loss, with Heavenly compassion we merit a strengthening beyond the bounds of nature. For Hashem has promised us that "it [the Torah] shall not be forgotten from the mouths of its [the people's] descendants."[4]

The Kabbalistic masters teach that the most powerful compassion of all is the compassion that emanates from *middas ha'din*, Hashem's attribute of justice.

The *Vilna Gaon* explains that it is specifically in the *berachah* of *Gevuros* that we say, "He sustains the living with kindness."[5] This is the secret of "*b'gevuros yesha yemino*—with might, His right hand will rescue." Seemingly, this is a contradiction, for *Gevuros* derives from *middas ha'din*, while *yemin*—the right—is the side of *middas ha'rachamim*! Rather, the greatest *rachamim*, compassion, is that which stems from *middas ha'din*.[6]

This, then, should be the focal point of educating children about the Holocaust. They must learn about the suffering and the destruction, but with care and with moderation, especially the youngsters whose soft hearts may find this too difficult to bear. We do not wish to arouse tortured questions and doubts in their young hearts, but rather to strengthen their *emunah* through demonstrating Heaven's compassion and the miraculous rejuvenation of Klal Yisrael and our acceptance of *ol malchus Shamayim* with renewed strength and vigor.

I have written briefly where there is much to expound upon at length. Again, I wish your honor success in all his ways. May you merit to sanctify Heaven's Name.

With love and admiration,
Asher Weiss

---

4   *Devarim* 31:21.
5   The second *berachah* of *Shemoneh Esrei*.
6   *Siddur HaGra, Avnei Eliyahu*, in *Lamenatzeach* of *Kedusha D'Sidra*. I have expounded on this at length in *Minchas Asher, Sichos al Hamoadim*, part 1, sec. 51, and in the *Zemiros L'Shabbos Minchas Asher*, pp. 23, 61.

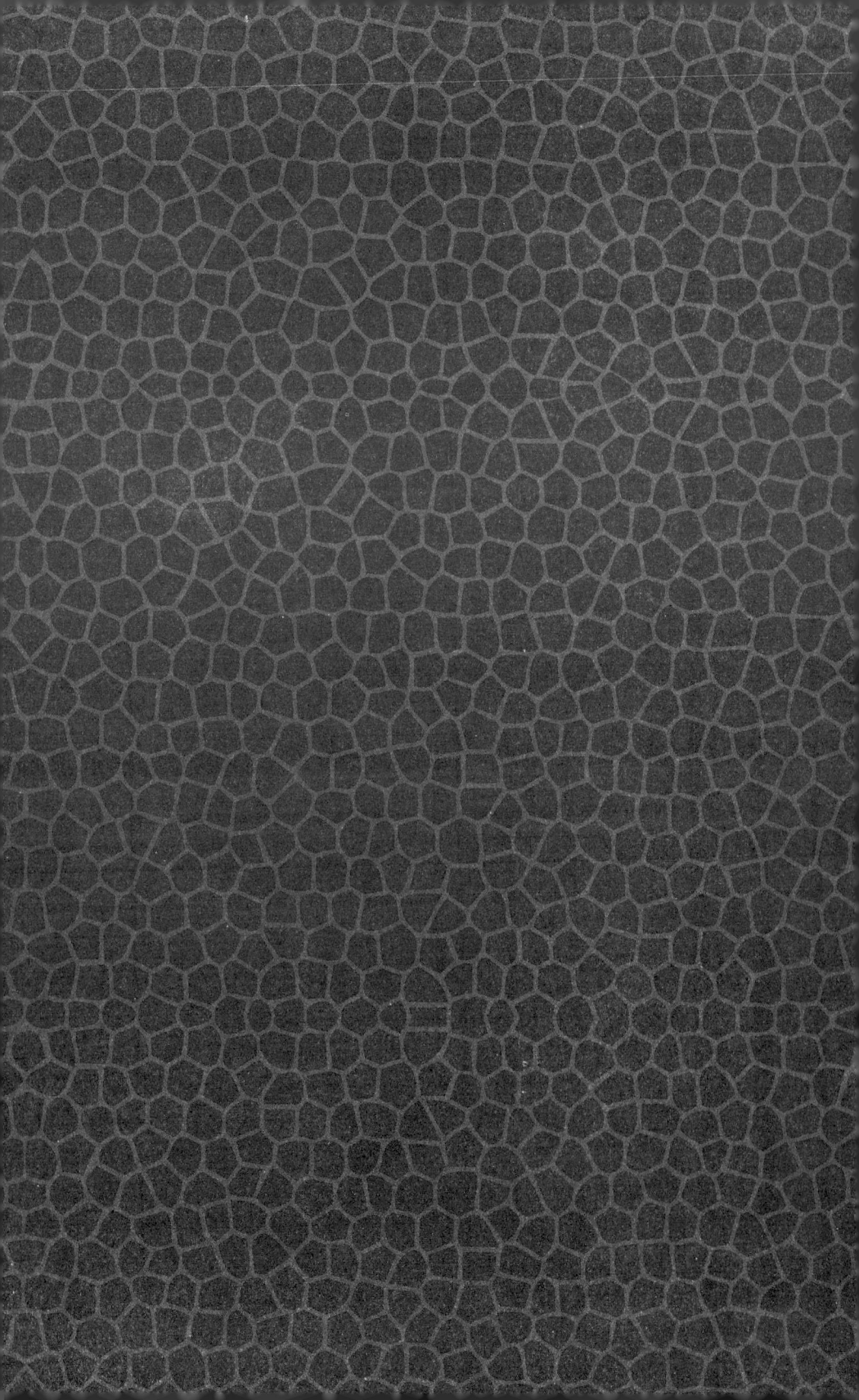